Over the Top with the Tartan Army

Active Service
1992-97

ANDREW McARTHUR

Luath Press Limited
EDINBURGH
www.luath.co.uk

ACKNOWLEDGEMENTS

AULD DAVIE KING shoulders a large part of the blame for my recruitment into the Tartan Army. Thereafter, I am indebted to many people for happy times and for their help in putting this book together: from Paddy McLaughlin for sparking the initial idea to Gus Clark who unwittingly suggested the title. It is not possible to list all of the people who have had a hand in the folly. Footsoldiers like Jimmy Cormack; Ian Russell; Calum Stewart; Alaister Corbett; Ian Munro; Tommy Madden; Wee Geordie; Kevin Lewis; Scott Kelly; Ronnie McDevitt; Craig McDowall; Billy McLeod; John Vila; Greg Kane; Craig Steven; Anneli Törblom; Gordon Hands; Alan Jamieson; Johnny Marr and Michael Roberts are a few of the many who provided tales and photos.

My good pal John Black, who has so far resisted the temptation to travel, also bears some responsibility by telling me that he found some of the early material amusing and then turning it into a play (*On Manoeuvres*) which was performed during Glasgow's 1997 Mayfest. Without his encouragement I would have probably done the sensible thing. Dair McGregor, Jimmy Briggs, Tommy Madden, Pete Martin and my mother forced themselves to read a draft of the book when it was even worse than it is now, yet failed to advise me abandon the project. My girlfriend, Bridget, also deserves special mention. A welcome home with open arms after every campaign can only be interpreted as encouragement. Thanks go to Rob Morrice, Pete Martin, Ben Craig, Young Steve, Mike Mystery, Paula McNally, Karen Pruce and Jim Hunter of SMARTS for design work on the cover and for help with promotion. As they say, never judge a book by its cover!

Thanks to *Scotland on Sunday* — Scotland's top sports newspaper — for providing all the photographs of famous people for the front cover from their photo library, to Graham Spiers — Scotland's top sports writer — for the foreword, and to Roben Antoniewicz photographer extraordinaire!

Gavin MacDougall of Luath Press deserves a special mention for a speedy turnaround following receipt of the draft manuscript. Once Luath got his teeth into the job, it was possible to foist the book on an unsuspecting public in advance of the World Cup in France. Please raise a glass to the late Albert Longstaff (the boy piper in *Brigadoon*) who taught Big Davie the pipes. Finally, I'd like to thank everyone who has ever pulled on a shirt for Scotland, and all who ever wished they had.

Andy McArthur
1 April 1998

ANDREW McARTHUR is a lapsed Dumbarton fan whose first experience of following Scotland abroad (apart from Wembley) was the World Cup finals in West Germany in 1974. He has never fully recovered. He has now reached a stage in his life when he should know better, but recently refused to celebrate his 40th birthday and eagerly awaits Scotland's next away game. He has somehow managed to balance the demands of active service in the Tartan Army with a testing career in the academic world. At the time of writing, the author lectures at a leading Scottish institution of higher education, but he has been assured by Tam Ritchie that there is a taxi job waiting for him in Stockport should he soon be in need of gainful employment. When Scotland are not playing away, he lives quietly and happily in the West End of Glasgow. He hardly ever goes out and has been teetotal since a bad experience with vodka after the game against Russia in Moscow in 1995. Two of the most gratifying things in his life are to see new faces appear at Scotland away games and to meet up again with friends whom he has travelled with on previous campaigns. He firmly believes that he will see Scotland lift the World Cup before he joins Jimmy Hill in Auld Nick's hot house.

DEDICATION

This book is dedicated to Thomas 'Wee Dougie' McTaggart
from the Renton who tells me he plans to follow
Scotland abroad when his Dad will let him go.

First Edition 1998
The paper used in this book is acid-free,
neutral-sized and recyclable.
It is made from low chlorine pulps produced in a
low energy, low emission manner from sustainable forests.
Printed and bound by
The Cromwell Press, Trowbridge.
Typeset in 11 point Bembo by
SMARTS, Edinburgh.

CONTENTS

UNION DES ASSOCIATIONS EUROPÉENNES DE FOOTBALL

TÉLÉPHONE 031/941 41 21
TÉLEX 912 037 UEF/CH
TÉLÉFAX 031/941 18 38

ADR TÉLÉGR UEFA
CASE POSTALE 16
CH-3000 BERNE 15

Autumn 1992

Dear Friend,

We should like to take this opportunity, on behalf of the UEFA Fair Play Panel, to extend our sincere congratulations to all of the Scottish football fans who travelled to Sweden and provided their team with such enthusiastic and good-natured support for all of its matches.

As a result of this outstanding behaviour, the Fair Play Panel decided that a special award should be presented to each of the Scottish fans who attended the matches. We would therefore be pleased if you would accept the enclosed cloth badge, which we are able to send to you as a result of the endeavours of the Scottish F.A., as a special memento of the event, and also as a token of UEFA's appreciation.

Although your team did not perhaps always achieve the results which you might have hoped for, the conduct of the Scottish fans was exemplary throughout the event, and the team can be truly proud of the backing which it received from its supporters. It is UEFA's hope that fans from other countries will be inspired by this example, and that they will in future give their teams the same loyal and uplifting support as you have given your team.

Many congratulations to you all once again, and may you continue to derive as much pleasure from the game of football as you obviously have done up until now.

President of UEFA

General Secretary of UEFA

Lennart Johansson

Gerhard Aigner

UEFA letter confirming the Tartan Army's ambassadorial status!

'AFTER A WHILE YOU FORGET HOW SICK YOU FEEL WHEN SCOTLAND GET BEAT.'

EVEN THE MOST SANE OF WITNESSES confesses it is a masochist's nightmare following Scotland. If that statement is a contradiction then all to the better – for it captures the essence of the Scotland supporter, suspended between the pleasure he desires and the pain he somehow revels in. I personally can vouch for this human habitat because I have seen it often at close quarters: Scotland supporters roistering through dark eastern European alleyways at night, a bottle and a song to hand, and a broad smile across the face, when the team have just been humped.

It seems to me that the Tartan Army are in various ways a loveable bunch of fools. I don't doubt that clever sociologists in redbrick colleges all over the shop will have numerous theories about social escapism and stress-release mechanisms to explain their behaviour. The facts remain that they lose a lot of money, and sometimes marriage contracts, to follow their national team around numerous doomed assignments and suffer severe headaches and vomiting in the effort. When real-life combat soldiers endure these symptoms, their circumstances are deemed to be ghastly. When the Tartan Army return home, broke and forlorn, they refer to it as great fun.

In recent years, to add to this merry bevvying culture, it seems to me two further traditions have emerged. The first is this daft legacy from foreign travel of Tartan Army footsoldiers falling in love. I use the verb 'to fall' correctly here because, more often than not, the image is of a tartan tommy falling off the edge of an empty bottle somewhere to slur some weak eulogies to a leggy Swede in a dank nightclub in Gothenburg. In some cases, the wonder is that she falls for it and gets married. This nonsense truly took off after the Argentinean fiasco in 1978. If there was one thing from that period that outdid fans with Ally MacLeod carpets, it was other Rabs and Boabs letting out great belches before announcing that they had just met the loves of their lives. Of course, the gemme was their true love, but some of these relationships are still enduring.

And the second emerging tradition is surely this business of 'the good behaviour' that seems to have broken out like a bad rash among Scotland supporters. I am not cynical about this, although this fine decorum is peculiarly Scottish, and, I might add, peculiarly Tartan Army. Not every nation of citizens would regard the public bevvying, swearing and farting (the latter with the kilt hoisted up for maximum effect) as the perfect symptoms of civic order. For a country such as ours, which in the 1970s was among the foremost exporters of hooliganism, there is also a hilarious smugness about this new development among the fans. They positively revel in it now. I remember someone once telling me Scottish supporters were 'being good out of sheer wickedness'. When they won that UEFA Good Supporters award in 1992, it was a bit like hearing of a bunch of alcoholics who had suddenly taken over the Temperance Society. I love the Scottish football fan, in particular his cheery deviousness!

They are also, of course, blessed with humour, one of the sharpest blades in the human arsenal, which makes the reading of this fine book all the more mirthful. In following Andy McArthur's chronicle through places like Moscow, Rome, Copenhagen and the Faroes, you are left once more feeling slightly proud that these stupid creatures are your own countrymen. I'm not one of those who goes to town on claims that we as a nation are truly unique, but we're still not bad for eccentric behaviour. When these Scotland supporters laugh at themselves, you can hear the guffawing for miles around. And much of the time they're broke. And most the time they're unwell. In one magical sentence, plucked from the middle of this tome, McArthur writes: 'People forget how sick they felt watching Scotland get beat'. But not sick enough, evidently, for the next campaign overland down to

Athens to take place. I commend this book to all football supporters who love the game and can't help laughing at, and loving a little bit of, themselves. Some of it is genuinely hilarious. After reading it, I have almost concluded that the most accurate assertion you could make of a Scotsman is that he will go anywhere and say anything for the sake of a trivial pleasure. Especially, it seems to me, if there might be a match ticket down the road.

Graham Spiers
Scotland on Sunday
Glasgow 1998

CHAPTER 1

GET A FEATHER TAE YER BUNNET, A KILT ABIN YER KNEE, ENLIST BONNIE LAD AND COME AWA WI ME

'WHAT DO YOU WANT FOR YOUR BIRTHDAY SON?' Auld Davie was standing in the doorway of my granny's living room in the high flats at Townhead in Glasgow. Davie appeared only now and again. Worked away a lot, usually in Germany building oil and chemical tanks. I didn't know my Uncle Davie too well at that time. But I'd heard that he was a bit of a character, liked a good bevvy, a bet and was no stranger to pandemonium.

This was mid October, 1973. The birthday in question was my 16th, but it was not for another 3 months. The last present I could recall getting from my Uncle Davie was a chess set. Wooden pieces in a light coloured wooden box with a sliding top. I think it's still around somewhere, or at least some of it will be. The chess set had been for my 6th or 7th birthday. I was never really very keen on chess, but the image of this wooden chess box was the only thing that jumped to mind as I struggled for a reply to Davie's question.

Before the living room door swung open to announce Uncle Davie, I'd been thinking about Joe's goal. I had been thinking about it for a few weeks. Joe's goal was the main topic of conversation with my school mates Stevie Newlands and Graham (Duck) Dick. Stevie, me and Duck were behind the goal as Joe Jordan's diving header hit the net and detonated the Hampden Roar. It was the beginning of many glorious years service from big Joe. Of more immediate cause for riotous celebration was that Joe had put Bonnie Scotland 2:1 up against the Czechs and into the World Cup finals in West Germany in June 1974.

1

Scotland in the World Cup Finals! That didn't figure at all on the landscape of my memory. Very different now when the prospect of Scotland's absence from the greatest show on earth is a justifiable cause for prolonged national mourning. From TV I could remember the glamour of Mexico in 1970 as the stunning Brazilians lifted the World Cup for the third time. So Scotland were going to the ball.

'It would be great to be there, eh Stevie. Imagine Scotland walking out against a team like that Brazil, Champions of the World.'

'I'd love to go and see Scotland in the World Cup, Uncle Davie.'

It just came out, relegating the chess set to oblivion. Thinking back I'm still surprised at myself. Maybe if I'd asked for a set of darts or a fishing rod my life would have been very different. But then again I was never that keen on darts or fishing. Maybe it was probably just a way of letting Davie know I'd been part of that great Wednesday night in September.

'If my horse comes up we'll go,' announced the figure in the doorway. I don't recall any more being said than that. Davie was gone. Over the next few months the nation's excitement about the World Cup grew, especially when the draw placed Scotland in the same section as Brazil.

'So we've actually got them Stevie. Do you think Pele will play? Let's get a big carry out and watch the game round at Duck's.'

Duck's mum was pretty easy going and probably wouldn't mind, given the occasion.

But it turned out to be Smoky Joe's, not Duck's, that was my local during the Finals. Smoky Joe's bar in Ruudesheim, West Germany. Turn right outside, go down the narrow cobbled street and you're soon on the banks of the River Rhine looking over towards Bingen. Alternatively, turn left, and in a couple of minutes you're climbing the steep slopes of the vineyards which supplied the unlabelled bottles of wine you could buy in Smoky Joe's and the other bars and kellers in Ruudesheim.

A few months later Davie had returned. Around March I think. Arriving unexpectedly, just as usual:

'Oh by the way, Andy, ma horse come up. See you in June.'

To say, Jessie, my mother, was delighted for me would not be exactly true. Auld Davie you see, is actually my mum's uncle, her mother's brother. Jessie had had plenty of exposure to her good uncle when she was in her late teens and early twenties and Davie not being that many years older. Mild dread was probably a more accurate description of her reaction. Although Davie was then pushing 50, age had not mellowed him. He's now in his early 70s and, as you read on, you'll find nothing has changed.

Jessie met us off the plane at Glasgow Airport when we returned from Frankfurt in June. She was getting a wee bit worried as most of the fans from our flight had already come through. I had lost sight of Davie for a few minutes, then spotted him going round on the baggage carrousel giving the few remaining fans waiting for their luggage one last rendition of *We'll Support You Evermore*. Jessie was very pleased to see us back almost in one piece. Even the stookie on my right arm that was doing a poor job of mending a broken finger coupled with the news that Davie had given away a treasured tammy that Jessie had borrowed from a work colleague to an Australian he'd met at the Brazil game could not dent her obvious delight, and surprise, that we'd (or, more accurately, that I'd) survived the ordeal. We'd come through our first campaign together. The first of many.

It was another 16 years before Auld Davie and me stood together again on a foreign terracing. Italia '90. I'd popped into the Vale Bar in Dundas Street, Glasgow the previous Christmas Eve. I'd got into the habit of drinking with Davie now and again by then and we'd been to a good few boxing matches together in the 80s - the Watt fights and wee Barry's emotional world title victory at Loftus Road in London. We'd become good pals.

Auld Davie: still fisting after all these years.

'Here's yer Christmas present,' I said, and laid a small parcel down on the bar. It didn't feel like a pair of socks or pants - the usual mindings. As Davie peeled off the paper a wee smile appeared. It was a *Teach Yourself Italian* phrase book.

By then the Tartan Army was a seasoned travelling support and the Jimmy Hill song had become a classic. Three successful World Cup qualifying campaigns had led the troops to the Argentine, Spain and Mexico and Mr Jimmy Hill, then a less well known English commentator who mistakenly labelled David Narey's glorious opening strike against Brazil in Seville a 'toe poke,' had seen to that. And we'd missed it all, at first hand that is.

Jimmy Cormack – looking for his other eye.

For growing numbers of Scottish fans there was more to live for than the Wembley weekend every two years. Bars in far away places like Israel, Iceland, South America and the other side of the former Iron Curtain had beckoned without the prospect of a hike in beer prices or a withdrawal of public transport on match day which had characterised London's response to the Scots fans. Supporters' attitudes and dress were also changing. Kilts, balmorals, glengarrys and pheasant feathers were much more common than they had been in West Germany.

Auld Davie and I had been missing from much of the action, but the stories still filtered back from folk I knew well, like Jimmy Cormack and Jim Manual from my home town, Dumbarton. Jimmy, who I've now travelled with several times and who we will meet again later in the book, still talks fondly about the Israel campaign in 1981, when Scotland emerged with a 1:0 victory over the the hosts in Tel Aviv on their way to the World Cup Finals in Spain 1982. With the exception of some sightseeing, like a visit to Jerusalem's Wailing Wall where a group of the

Tartan Army bemused onlooking Jews and tourists by swaying backwards and forwards singing 'We are wailing, we are wailing...' (to Rod Stewart's *Sailing*), much of the chaos centred on the Gypsy Bar in Tel Aviv. This bar was the scene of a bizarre wedding ceremony. An account of the event made prime spot on page 2 of the serious daily broadsheet, the *Jerusalem Post*. The article, entitled *Just a wee bit of a Highland fling*, was written by a correspondent called Tony Kutner. Here it is reproduced below in full:

Upwards of 30 beers a head were being downed in the Gypsy Bar when I arrived yesterday. Everybody was hysterical as Frank (The Wank) from Clydebank declared that he intended to be married right there in the middle of the bar. A few moments later, a drunk with tattoos on his naked torso staggered over me in an effort to reach the wedding which had now begun amid the sweat, noise and general hysteria.

I pushed my way to the scene just in time to hear the Reverend George Guiness declaring Frank and his woman, Morag, man and wife. The good reverend was suitably dressed for the occasion in kilt, Scottish flag around the shoulders and a tam o' shanter on his head. All of this of course was another excuse for more drink and hilarity. Rod Stewart was blaring on the video and the Scots were in ecstasy. A worried bar owner glanced about uneasily as the place shook to the rhythm of the dancing, flailing bodies. The Scotland-Israel football match hadn't even begun yet.

Jacobite John said this trip has been fairly tame for him, after having hitch-hiked to see Scotland play in the World Cup finals in Argentina in 1978. He has been sleeping on the beaches here and in other people's bedrooms. On his first night he was an advance member of the Scottish Footballer's Association Party at the Tel Aviv Hilton. Now there was less room than ever because men were dancing romantically in each other's arms. They said that Israeli girls were beautiful, but that they could wait until after the match. The video now featured Glasgow singer Lena Martell, whose song according to the fans, went 'One goal at a time, sweet Kenny'.

It becomes ever more apparent that football is not simply a game to the Scots. To the 2,000 who flew into Israel to see the match, it is a moral crusade to see their heroes win, with drink, sex and singing taking an equally important place. The Scots have actually caused very little trouble in Israel. This they attribute to the mature attitude of the police, who have handled most situations with tact and patience. They have, in fact, nothing but praise for the Israelis, whom they have found helpful and exceedingly warm. We finally left for the match in convoy, one of my party leaving his lunch down the side of the taxi while his friend told him not to worry because he would soon have some good hot coffee and 'tacheenay' inside him. At the game, the Scots sang and drank, my associates having successfully smuggled in 15 bottles of beer. As usual, all tried to sing their team to success, the Scottish roar being fully apparent after the one goal of the match. They had come from all over Scotland, travelling on overnight trains without much sleep. Some had arrived to spend the whole night in the bar, fortifying themselves for the great effort of will ahead. (Tony Kutner, *Jerusalem Post*, p. 2, 21 February 1981).

One travelling fan had no chance of making Frank's wedding. He had mistakenly flown to Cairo rather than Tel Aviv. Not fully appreciating the political sensitivities of the Middle East, its geography and having lost his passport, he thought he'd just 'nip across this here stretch of sand'. He was surprised to find himself challenged and detained by Arab security forces. He eventually arrived in Tel Aviv the day after the game and having given an account of his troubles to fellow fans in the Gypsy Bar he was promptly christened the Desert Fox.

Jim Manual proved to be a rich and amusing source of tales. Over the five years up to and including Italia '90 Manual appeared at every Scotland away game when he should have been appearing in front of a class of business studies pupils at his local high school. Jim was a larger than life character who rode his luck for a few years. I believe that he is currently seeking his fortune overseas and has little opportunity to follow Scotland these days, but let's concentrate on Jim's happier times during active service.

The tale of Manual's Mexico campaign begins in the Stags Head pub in Dumbarton. Jim was a hell of a man for Trivial Pursuit machines. These ask you a question in an area such as sport, entertainment, or whatever, and give you a list of possible answers to chose from. Get one wrong and you lose. The more you get right, the more difficult the questions become and the shorter the time you have to register your answer. Well Jim was shit hot and his name continually topped the list of highest scorers. The distributors of the game were running a competition.

The best in the country would win a trip to Mexico. Manual made the national finals in Edinburgh and was the first to go, out of a group of around seventy local area champions. When Jim returned to the competition hall after the afternoon in the pub his score had not been bettered and a free trip to the World Cup in Mexico was his for the taking.

However, there still remained his work to contend with, the school year being poorly synchronised with the greatest show on earth. This posed Jim no immediate problem as he suffered the first of a long line of back complaints which laid him off on the sick. On arriving at Glasgow Airport en route to Mexico, Jim was met by an interviewer and cameraman from the *Daily Record* wanting his story. Jim couldn't take the chance that his boss might be a *Daily Record* reader and, sadly, was unable to assist. The picture which appeared the next day on the front page of the Record shows an anonymous character, face completely hidden by a large sombrero, under the headline 'Mystery Man goes to Mexico'.

Jim's back ailment became chronic and was to see him good for many a game abroad. Until, that is, Limassol. Scotland carried the luck of the Irish during the game against the Cypriots in February, 1989. The East German referee (Siegfried Kirschen) must have had a Scotland jersey on under his shirt as he played a full seven minutes injury time with dubious justification. These seven minutes were enough for Richard Gough to head the all important winner that gave Scotland a 3:2 victory and provoked riots in the stadium.

Manual was not blessed with the same outrageous good fortune when he next showed up at school. Invited to the Head's room with the union rep also in attendance he soon got wind of what was going down.

'Look here Jim,' said the Head. 'This is a list of Scotland's away fixtures over the past five years. And this is your sickness record. Strange, isn't it? The dates are an exact match.'

Manual immediately conceded that this was indeed the strangest thing, but it was pure coincidence nevertheless.

'OK then, where were you last week?' The inquisition began. 'Come Jim, admit it, you were at the game. We know you were there. It'll be better for you if you come clean.' But Jim stuck by his story. He had been incapacitated once again by his chronic back problem. Then the Head got up, went to the door and wheeled in a TV and video monitor.

'This is your last chance Jim. Were you at the game?' Still Jim refused to budge. The video was switched on to show recorded highlights of the game.

Now you are possibly saying to yourself that surely this was when Jim should have cut his losses and declared his hand. But Jim thought he had an ace up his sleeve. He couldn't have been recognised. He had had the common sense to wrap his Scotland scarf round his face during the game just in the off chance the TV cameras caught him in the crowd. They must be mistaking someone else for him.

'Still insisting you weren't there?'

'I was at home flat on my back. How many times do I need to tell you?' Jim was growing in confidence now.

The Head fast forwarded the tape. The game was now finished and people were being interviewed about the result. Jim relaxed. Then the camera switched to the streets of Limassol. Drunken, happy faces. Tartan Army singing and dancing. And there's Jim there, smack bang in the middle of a line of fans dancing a jig for the cameras.

Amazingly Jim's employment at the school was not terminated. Not then anyway. Departure came a bit later. But Jim's back problem had been cured for good.

'No luck Jim. Where are you watching the game tomorrow?' was the gist of the common room conversation on the Tuesday afternoon before another Scotland away game. At this time Jim managed a local amateur football team and occasionally joined in the training. On the Wednesday morning he turned up at work with his leg heavily strapped. He was as white as a sheet and clearly in great discomfort as he hobbled around the school on a pair of crutches. Colleagues were genuinely concerned.

'I done my ankle at training last night. They think it might be a hairline fracture.' But Jim waved off all suggestions that he should go home, a heroic which only provoked more attention and demands that he should call it a day. It was not until the Head appeared and insisted he take the rest of the day off that Jim reluctantly conceded and a taxi was called.

A few teachers and pupils witnessed Jim shuffling towards the taxi, and the agonised expression on his face as he bent into the vehicle. They did not know that they were watching a beautifully delivered and timed acting performance. But Jim was not going for an Oscar. He was going for a midday flight. The last scene in the show was reserved for the taxi driver who got the shock of his life when they reached the airport. Helping Jim from the back seat he went to hand him the crutches.

'Naw, just launch them' said Jim as he grabbed his bag and sprinted off in the direction of the departure lounge.

Manual hung on in Acapulco after Scotland, and most of the fans, had departed. A late evening stroll in the neighbourhood of the hotel was now quieter and slightly more threatening than it had been a few days earlier. Jim was surprised, but not shocked, when he noticed a couple of legs sticking upwards out of a bush.

'The poor bugger's been mugged', he thought. He went over to see if the person was still alive. But he did get a shock when he got to the bush. Attached to the legs was a bare arse. The guy was upside down, but Jim couldn't make out his face as it was covered with a kilt. Uprighting his fellow straggler Jim found him too drunk to talk or walk. So it was over the shoulder and back to the hotel.

It wasn't till morning that the visitor began to stir. The painful regaining of consciousness was followed by some basic stocktaking – 'Where the fuck am'a?… How did I get here?… Thanks, who are you?'.

Jim told the stranger he lived in Dumbarton. It turned out that the guy, who introduced himself as Jimmy Thorburn, a life long Queen of the South fan from Castle Douglas, had lived in Dumbarton for a few years in the sixties and early seventies.

'Where abouts did you stay?' Jimmy asked.

'Leverford Terrace', said Manaul.

'What! That's where I stayed', says Jimmy. 'Do you know Andy McArthur? He used to live in No 2, the same close as me'.

'Sure', says Jim, 'He's in my football team.' I just had a pint with him the night before I left Scotland.' I hadn't seen Jimmy Thorburn for years. Small world indeed.

Manual and Jimmy Cormack both delight in another incident which took place a few days before in Acapulco. Scottish and English fans had been together for around a week in the town. They were not exactly 'together'. The Tartan Army relaxed, got bevvied and played the locals at football while our southern neighbours got pished but made a general nuisance of themselves. The English were due to move out and had hired half a dozen coaches to take them to Mexico City for the game against Argentina. It was a journey of around six or seven hours over the mountains.

One anonymous wee fella had been in the company all week but had said virtually nothing. Quiet as a mouse, Jimmy recalls. Just seemed to be happy listening wide-eyed to the crack. For this reason it struck Jimmy as odd to see the guy deep in conversation with a large group of English fans drinking nearby, killing time before their coaches arrived. Maybe this was him just coming out of his shell. But why the English? Anyway Jimmy got back to his beer and thought no more about the strange scene. About half an hour later the bloke returned to the company of the Scots fans and resumed his silent vigil.

Time was now pressing and the English fans were getting more and more agitated by the minute. Pacing up and down the street, constantly checking their watches, asking each other if they had the right pick up point, and cursing the 'spicks' for their crap time keeping. One of the Scots lads asked if it was not time they were away to the game.

'We're waiting for these stupid Mexican bastards to turn up with our coaches'. At that point the wee guy leaned forward into the company, 'They're no going anywhere. Ah cancelled their coaches'. A cruel trick you could say, but unwittingly he had done them a favour. For had they made it to Mexico City they would have had to endure a real shafting at 'the Hand of God and the head of Maradona'.

The first time Auld Davie and I travelled with Jimmy

Cormack was for the Finland game in Helsinki in 1994: a fine 2:0 victory for the Scots in our ultimately successful bid to reach the 1996 European Championships in England. However, by then the idea of a book about the Tartan Army had already occurred to me. The idea first came to mind over a few beers with Paddy McLaughlin and some of the other Dunfermline boys outside a small café in Gothenburg in '92. I think it was the day after our 2:0 defeat at the hands of West Germany which meant we were out of Euro '92, but not before Scotland hammered three past the CIS without reply a few days later.

Paddy had just finished a tale about himself and his pal Brian Simpson during Italia '90 when they awoke late one morning in Rimini on Italy's Adriatic coast to confront a major logistical problem. Stretching away the cobwebs of a hangover as the sun streamed through the bedroom window, Paddy blinked with disbelief at the bedside clock. Bolt upright he shot. They had missed their coach to Turin which was inconveniently located on the other side of the country. The next half hour was occupied by a frantic assessment of their transportation options. Train, taxi, hired car. All no good. It was mid-day. Turin was six hours drive away and the kick-off was in 3 hours.

They were slumped at the hotel bar as the full horror of their predicament sunk in. For Paddy, a veteran drummer of many campaigns, this was a disaster. Only a few days before he had led a march of thousands through the streets of Genoa to the Luigi Ferrara stadium to face Sweden in a thrilling 2:1 victory for Scotland. The police took Paddy to be the main man and sought his advice as they stopped and

Paddy drumming in Gothenburg.

11

redirected city centre traffic to let this huge singing throng of fans snake its way through central Genoa.

'I can't believe this, we've missed the game', groaned Paddy.

After a few minutes of silence Brian slipped away, returning about half an hour later.

'We'll not miss the game', he announced, 'I've hired us a helicopter. It'll be here shortly'. As they made their way through the café area outside the hotel they passed a wee guy from Ayr, another stranded fan, who'd been in their company the night before.

'It's great to see you lads. I thought I'd be watching the game on ma todd'. He completed the trio.

The troops wanted to be dropped at the game but the pilot said that this was impossible as there was no designated landing spot near the Stadio Della Alpi in Turin. The nearest put-down spot was the Fiat plant, some 17 kilometres from the ground.

'Can you organise us transportation from there?' Brian asked.

'Certainly, anything you like' said the pilot. 'In that case, order us a limo.'

The landing was amusing. The helicopter descended to a spot in front of the canteen where the limousine was already waiting. A couple of hundred workers stood close by or watched from inside the canteen.

The Tartan Army in Sweden for Euro '92: the best 'holiday' ever.

'It looked like they were expecting Madonna or Rod Stewart' said Paddy. 'You should have seen their faces when it was three drunks in full regalia, one with spats and a side drum, that poured into the limo.'

This was just one of many gems I'd heard recounted during Euro '92 in Sweden.

'You know Paddy, this is the best holiday I've ever been on,' I said.

Paddy, feigning horror, stared down at his snare drum, then declared, 'For fuck sake Andy, you're not on holiday. You're on National Service. You're in Sweden with the Tartan Army.'

Yet the book idea remained no more than an idea at that time. But further encouragement was received when we played a friendly against Holland, losing 3:1 (but savouring Duncan Shearer's first goal for his country) in Utrecht in 1994. Holland were going to the finals of the World Cup in the USA. Scotland weren't, although the Shetland boys from the island of Yell did. It was back in Amsterdam after the game that I first met Wee Geordie. Wee Geordie is a Galloway man, a passionate Jacobite and bon viveur who lives in a London squat with an ageing Rastafarian who he refers to as 'Uncle Henry'. Geordie appears at least 10 years older than his birth certificate claims, and looks as though he hasn't washed for half as long. A fine footsoldier, he was enthusiastic about the book idea. I mentioned I'd spotted him at a previous World Cup qualifying game in Rome (a 3:1 defeat in October 1993) with a group that looked as though they had just walked off Culloden Battlefield. This launched him into a couple of hilarious tales of what this group of Jacobites had got up to during that particular campaign.

Geordie's group had driven over in a couple of vans. Pickle, of the Peterhead Psycho Crew, whose dreadlocks (at that time) hung half way down his back, drove a vehicle which carried, amongst others, his pals

Pickle's sporran made from his own dreadlocks.

Gudge and Mad Dog McLeod from Arbroath. Pickles no longer has his famous dreadlocks. They have been cut and stuck onto an old sporran which is proudly worn at every Scotland away game. Pickles hooked up with a second van from London which included Chiz (another Arbroath ex-pat), Eddie O'Gorman and Ally Cairns the piper. Knowing that Charles Edward Stuart lies buried in the Vatican, advance plans were made to pay their respects and a wreath of white roses and heather was commissioned from an Italian flower shop in Chelsea. By the time the wreath reached Rome it looked more like a ring of barbed wire, but it would still serve its purpose.

Now the Vatican is not the easiest place to get into. Affluent American tourists were being turned away by the Swiss Guard because they were wearing shorts. The kilted Jacobites, with Doc Martin boots, old piper jackets, beards and long hair exemplified by Pickle had no problems. Behind the pipes, as they marched straight past the Swiss Guard and into the heart of the Vatican, Ally the piper changed from a traditional air and broke into a rendition of *The Sash*. Having laid the wreath at Bonnie Prince Charlie's grave, it proved more difficult to get out of the Vatican than it had been getting in.

Jacobites paying their respects at Bonnie Prince Charlie's grave in the Vatican, Rome.

'We'd attracted the attention of a lot of tourists', Geordie recalled, 'they were all wanting to take photographs. We could hardly get out of the place.'

Wee Geordie followed up the Vatican tale with a charming story I'm very fond of. Here it is in his own words:

Stevie Winn was staggering back to the campsite early in the morning after Scotland's 3:1 defeat in the Olympic Stadium. On the walk back from Ostia train station he felt that he was being followed. He looked back, but could see nothing in the darkness. Back at the tent something pressed against his leg. It was a wee fat black dog. After giving the mutt a cold tin of ravioli and plenty of fresh water he retired.

Late in the morning the early risers found the dog sleeping in the tent on a Saltire flag. With the smell of food wafting about, the wee dog awoke and decided that breakfast looked an easy bet from this motley group of men in skirts. Being a friendly fellow, nobody could refuse him. Then he showed his gratitude by joining in the game of football, displaying those dazzling Latin skills that had wiped the floor with Scotland the night before. Once Stevie revived, all was explained.

Our convoy was leaving for home that day so we drove to Ostia to try and find the dog's owner. At the train station café, a buxom friendly woman who loved the bagpipes so much that she supplied the company with unlimited free wine, told us that the dog was a stray. She had been feeding him on scraps for a couple of weeks.

A 'council' was then convened to consider what to do with the four legged Roman refugee. The dog couldn't be left where he was. So far he had been lucky to survive so close to a busy dual carriageway. The council had continued into the night when fierce argument broke out. One of the Peterhead Crew suggested that the dog would be a valuable food source on the long penniless road home, a motion seconded by two of the London Scottish regiment of foot, one of whom also thought that the animal's hide would make an excellent sporran. This idea was quickly howled down by threats of violence from Mad Dog McLeod who had taken a liking to the dog. Mad Dog's sister worked in a vet surgery back in Arbroath, so he phoned her and ask how much it would cost for quarantine to bring the dog back to Scotland. The sum of at least six hundred pounds was an insurmountable obstacle.

Then Gudge suggested we drive home via St Tropez in the South of France and look up Bridgitte Bardot who runs a shelter for dogs and cats who are down on their luck. If Ms Bardot had no room in her sanctuary, then we would try and nip her for the money to pay for the dog's quarantine.

The next morning two vans, fourteen men, one dog (by this time christened Caesar) departed Italy for the sun-kissed beaches of the French Riviera. We arrived in Monte Carlo at around 10am and stopped for coffee, petrol and to change drivers. Then we pressed on for St Tropez, but with the sun beating into the vans and with several people suffering from hangovers and runny bottoms (a result of too much cheap plonk), we decided to stop at the next town for a break. As the drivers had a kip, some of us went to find a vet in a bid to uncover Ms Bardot's exact whereabouts, leaving Ally Cairns to tune up and try his hand at busking in this well to do area. We found a vets at the other side of town, but to our disgust it was closed.

Back at the vans we found Ally talking to a stranger. While he was tuning his pipes in a park, a head popped up from behind a hedge and said, 'Are ye trying tae strangle a cat there son?' It was a guy, John from Kintyre, who worked as a gardener for a wealthy

Chiz picks up another real dog.

Swedish family. Fortunately they were away on holiday and we were invited up to the house for a drink where we indulged in some excellent wine from the well-stocked cellar. We explained our dilemma with Caesar and asked his advice. He confirmed that the vet would keep him for a short time, but, if no one came to take him, Caesar would be destroyed. Mad Dog was not amused. However, he also informed us that this town, Beaulieu-sur-Mer, was full of animal lovers. Someone might be found who would take such a good-natured dog as Caesar. The next morning we set off with the piper at our head blasting out *Flower of Scotland* alongside Caesar who now looked resplendent in a McLeod of McLeod tartan collar Mad Dog had cut from his scarf. After half an hour asking bemused locals if they wanted a dog, a lady from a very fashionable boutique approached. She had two very presentable poodle bitches who looked well-pampered and cared for in her shop. She wasn't too keen on owning another dog but promised to look after him until she found an owner. If attempts failed, then she would keep him herself rather than see him destroyed. Caesar by this time, showing his instinct for self-preservation, was already inside the boutique lying on the floor with the two lady poodles. It was time for us to leave and we tried to bid Caesar farewell, but he was far too busy sniffing to notice.

If any reader gets to the South of France, then by all means try and visit Beaulieu-sur-Mer, a small town between Monaco and Nice, and look Caesar up. There on the sea front, alongside the main Casino there is an expensive fashionable boutique. There, also, hopefully you will find him, still in his home made tartan collar living the life of a playboy. Caesar - the Tartan Army's mascot on the Italian job!

We will meet some of the above characters again during the book. Having travelled to almost all of the away games in recent years, Auld Davie and I have got to know many of the hard core fans well. Even over a period of just a few years we have noticed a number of changes in the Tartan Army. Sure there are still real veterans, like Joe Gibson from Glasgow (living in Crawley), who are still travelling. Joe's first Scotland game outside of mainland Britain was a 3:0 defeat by Italy in Naples in 1965. To get to Argentina in '78, Joe borrowed £3,000 from the Royal Bank of Scotland and still owed several hundred when he returned seeking a further loan for the '82 World Cup in Spain.

'Just top it up,' Joe told his bank manager, 'I'll soon sort you out when I get back.' Even with stalwarts like Joe Gibson, faces come and go as even some of the most committed fans step down for a while due to work pressures, family commitments or other mishaps. Mad Dog, for example, enjoyed a spell of semi-retirement in 1997, before his return to active service in time for France '98.

The Tartan Army is also becoming more organised. A noticeable recent development has been the growth of regional networks of fans. John Grigor from Ayr has a long standing network who have travelled with him under the auspices of 'Scotland Abroad' for many years. Similarly, the Partick Thistle International Supporters Section and the Perth Mob have a fairly long pedigree. But more recent supporters' clubs have emerged. In addition to the well established London Scottish (Lunnainn Albannaich) and the Edinburgh Tartan Army, new groups have been formed in Fife, the North of Scotland, the Highlands and the West of Scotland. These clubs are all helping to attract new supporters interested in following Scotland abroad and to introduce them to more seasoned campaigners.

The regional groups all know each other well and joint travelling arrangements between us are very common. Both the London and the Edinburgh troops have their own newsletter, the Edinburgh version lifting the phrase *Just One Chance'* from the film *Braveheart* for its title. They also have their own tee-shirts, as do some of the other clubs. The shirts of the London Scottish, for example, have a motif on the front which shows the rampant lion of Scotland giving the three passive lions of England a hard time. But it is the back of the London Scottish tee-shirts which are especially memorable. The ones made up for Euro '96 read:

Scots Invasion of England
1297 Wallace
1328 Bruce
1745 Bonnie Prince Charlie
1996 Tartan Army

Great stuff. It would be hard to better that. But the club's new shirt for 1997 had a good try at upsetting the natives one more time. On this occasion the back read:

Scotland's Players of the Year
'86 – Maradona
'88 – Van Basten
'90 – Pearce/Waddle
'92 – Brolin
'93 – Koeman
'96 – Southgate

Another recurring characteristic of the Tartan Army on manoeuvres is an aversion to short trips and direct travel. Rather than elect for the easiest route it is common for fans to make their way through several countries en route to a game. It is not unusual for fans to move through around half a dozen countries during a single trip. Campaigns lasting less than a week are the exception for many of the regular travelling support. One of the great things about following Scotland is the places you see and the people you meet. The football is important, but there is much more to it all than that.

The Tartan Army is now known, and remembered fondly, around a substantial part of the globe. Its institutional existence was further strengthened late in 1997 when brothers Ian and Alan Adie from Glasgow registered the phrase 'Tartan Army' as a Trade Mark and created a Tartan Army Tartan.

In this book we will journey to places like Russia, the Faroe Islands, Sweden, Monaco, Denmark, America, Estonia, Latvia,

Monaco, France, Finland and Belarus. The tales move onwards from the Tartan Army's celebrated participation in Euro '92 in Sweden. Most of the stories in this book are drawn from Scotland's qualifying games leading up to the European Championships in England in 1996 and the World Cup in France in 1998, but there is still the opportunity for fans to recall some memorable tales from earlier campaigns. There is not the space in this book to introduce you to all of the fans Auld Davie and I have

Ma Baker's Bar, Helsinki: the Tartan Army turning Finland into Funland.

met and will always remember. But on these trips we will be meeting some of the hardened footsoldiers from the greatest travelling support the World has ever seen.

Perhaps it is appropriate to round off this Chapter with a comment from young Derek Madden, one of the Partick Thistle International Supporters Section and who now travels regularly with his father Tommy who has been a big help in putting this book together. Derek is representative of much of the younger, hard core support. His first away game was in Spain in 1982 as a 12 year old, but it is really only since the 1992 European Championships in Sweden that he has been become a fully fledged footsoldier. I ask him why he follows Scotland. A daft question maybe, but his response is illuminating:

'What makes me a footsoldier, returning again and again to the fields of battle? The company is stupendous. There is no bigotry or old firm shite. We are a formidable army, maybe the only army in the world whose only weapon is their voices. Every so often a hack writes derogatory comments about us, but we don't care. And by the way hacks, your secrets about what you get up to are safe with us! As a final comment let me say to anyone reading this, take one trip, get kilted up, let it all hang free and find out what it is like to follow Scotland abroad.'

Thanks Derek. Now let's get on with the tales.
Now, read on for Scotland!

CHAPTER 2

DISPATCHES FROM THE RUSSIAN FRONT

SCOTLAND'S VENTURE INTO THE FORMER SOVIET UNION in late March 1995 was rewarded with more success than that afforded to the other half of the Auld Alliance under Napoleon some years earlier. Thankfully the early Spring fixture avoided the savage Russian winter that also brought Hitler's invading forces to their knees. The Tartan Army's march on Moscow found a nation in transition – a kind of 'Wild East' where a pervading feeling of danger kept our wits more acutely honed than the deluge of vodka should have permitted. A few of the troops admitted to being glad to see the back of the place, but as we withdrew with a valuable and unexpected point in our back pockets I doubt any of us would have missed what was a memorable campaign.

Auld Davie and I travelled down to London on the overnight train from Glasgow on Friday in the company of Davie Pollock who'd been with us at Italia '90. During the several hours we had to kill at Heathrow Airport we shared many beers with numerous contingents of fans who were catching flights before us. Some, like us, were flying direct to Moscow. Others were taking less direct routes. Amsterdam, Helsinki and Tallinn all figured in the list of first stop destinations.

The troops heading to Finland and Estonia were bound for a big party in Tallinn on the Saturday night, before embarking on a massive train journey the 800 or so miles to Moscow. It is always great to see so many weel kent faces at the start of a campaign. It gives you the chance to say the kind of farewell you wanted to at the end of the previous trip but couldn't because of health problems. Wee Hamish was there too, the Tartan Teddy that travels with Jim Todd, one of Grigor's Mob, and dresses in an identical red tartan suit. It's rumoured that the bear has been to more away games than Jim. Hard to believe as the pair seem inseparable. It's also said that the bear knows more about football, a more plausible claim altogether. Hamish was looking well and relaxed as he sat upright in an airport trolley listening to Corries' songs belting out from a ghetto blaster at his right ear.

Hamish holding up Jim.

Looking back on Moscow it was, quite simply, a string of bizarre incidents, large and small, but all bizarre nonetheless. A city of strange happenings and stranger people. The first Russian we spoke to, certainly the least threatening and possibly the most intelligent, was an 11 year old lad called Alex Vospiansky who was travelling back from a year out at school in England. Small, dark haired, bright eyed and very smart in his green school uniform, Alex spoke better English than any of the fans on the plane. Not that this bothered us in the least, but he also gave the impression of being vastly more intelligent, which was a little disconcerting. This impression was borne out when someone asked Alex what Russia was like since the fall of communism. Pausing now and again to make sure the Tartan half wits were following, Alex spoke about the problems of spiralling inflation, growing discontent with free markets and the possibilities of the military seizing power if the politicians could not bring about some stability. The inquisitors quickly claimed fatigue and played possum for the last hour or so of the flight. A sensible strategy. For apart from minimising embarrassment, very little sleep was on the cards for the week ahead.

On a different flight another 11 year old was also leaving a lasting impression. Young Murray from Dunfermline, on his way to his first Scotland game, treated the flight to a demonstration of his skill as a piper as he made his way up and down the aisle and into the cockpit to give the flight crew and passengers renditions of *Scotland the Brave* and other favourites. Murray's routine was the same on the flight home although the audience was a little more subdued. He was over with Paddy McLaughlin and Brian Simpson, the same pair who hired the helicopter to get them to the Brazil game in Italy back in '90. Paddy had also brought the wee man's mum to make sure the young piper would be OK and that nothing would interfere with his disposition to do the business. As it happened, bringing the maw was unnecessary, but Cathy made a fine contribution to the company.

Murray was already mature beyond his years and fitted in no problem as the Tartan Army moved through its manoeuvres. That's not to say he didn't mature in leaps and bounds. Moscow probably dumped a decade of experience on the young lad's shoulders.

This was possibly running through Paddy's mind during a farewell pint in the bar at Gatwick Airport on the way back when he sighed, 'Well now Murray, what are you going to tell your pals back at school when they ask you what you did during your Easter holidays?'

Many of the troops had arranged their travel through Intourist, a London-based agency, formerly the official travel arm of the old Soviet Union, but now trying to trade independently. Intourist had strongly advised pre-booking coaches and cars to avoid any difficulties getting from Sheremetyevo II Airport into the city, like getting ripped off by airport-based taxis. Of course, on arrival there was no sign of the pre-booked vehicles. More disappointingly, the bleak airport bar proved to be a dry zone as it refused to accept dollars, insisting on roubles, or 'rubbles' as they quickly became known. Meanwhile the troops had begun to improvise and alternative transportation into the city was negotiated. After about three-quarters of an hour attracting hungry leers from some desperate looking characters (Russians, not fellow Scots) a bus and some cars were secured and we were off. On the way out of the airport car park, Yuri, who had made the arrangements, pointed to a bus on its way in. It was one of the pre-booked efforts but our wheels were already in motion.

During the 1990s the Baltic Sea has seen quite a lot of the Tartan Army and was used by some of the travelling support who favoured a more circuitous route to Moscow. The attractions of the sail between Stockholm (Sweden) and Helsinki (Finland), and from there to Tallinn (Estonia), which involves around 24 hours of serious partying, was sufficient attraction to set the Tartan Army seabound. These Baltic sails also have a high recreational purpose for Scandinavians who are fond of a wee swally and think nothing of sailing off into the inhospitable Baltic for hours of cheap bevvy. Some of the crafts look like floating high rise flats, with multiple decks devoted to drinking and merriment.

A group of the Tartan Army, which included Russell Ritchie, a fisherman from Anstruther, was sailing from Stockholm to Helsinki en route to Moscow. They walked into the disco bar wishing that they were just hitting their kip, but hearts soared when they saw the bevvy of talent surrounding them.

'It's going to be a good night after all' announced Russell. But their hearts fell when five fine looking guys with bulging muscles walked in a few minutes later. Hearts fell further when another five of the same soon joined them. These were shortly followed by another five plus one wee ugly guy. The musclemen turned out to be the Chippendales from Texas. The ugly bloke was their bus driver, a wee fella from Glasgow.

Russell recalls a great night. The Texans couldn't believe the antics and stamina of the Tartan Army who danced and threw the girls around for several hours without remission. But the few hard days that the troops had already put under their belts must have taken its toll. For at the end of the night it was the Chippendales that walked off with the pick of the ladies. The Scots, including the bus driver, were consigned to the bar for the rest of the sail.

Russell's group hooked up with the party in Tallinn and were part of the division who boarded the train to Moscow. This was, by all accounts, a train journey with a difference. The lads trudged through the snow onto the train. All train passengers had been advised by officials about how to behave: basically to get into your compartment, keep the doors locked and place a rolled up, wet towel along the bottom of the cabin door. Violent robbery is a not uncommon and the wet towel is a precaution against gassing – a favourite tactic used by train bandits before smashing into cabins and relieving passengers of their belongings. Needless to say the forty-odd Tartan Army who made the journey did not stick strictly to this advice. The cabin doors were left wide open. Doors could not be shut for prostrate bodies lying half-in half-out of the cabins.

A large female guard was doing her best to shift the bodies into cabins in some orderly fashion, and was trying, with little success, to rouse them with a volley of jabs and kicks.

'Away and attend to them next door,' gesticulated Gus (The Cobra) Clark. He could hear his advice had been acted upon when the scream came. The scream announced that the guard had come face to face with Kevin Lewis, Big Bruce and several others who were lying in the kind of upside down heap that only Scottish fans seem to be able to sculpture – the defining characteristic of which is the kilt over the head and bare arses staring skyward. But the lady was still not through. A newspaper was acquired, set alight and tossed onto the pile of bodies.

By the time the train reached the border the troops were awake and digging around for passports. Bruce's attracted more attention than the others, being the only old black version in the company and sporting a thin face with long hair – an image which bore no resemblance to the live head on display. Peering intently at the passport and then again to Bruce, the border guard announced in Russian something sounding like 'ah, familiar cock.' The eruption of laughter during what was normally a sombre occasion had the guards reaching for their guns. Even so, the train contingent entered Russia in one piece.

One trooper who did not enter Russia was (Lucky) Murray Frazer from Aberdeen. In fact Lucky's run of misfortune had started a few months earlier than that. When I met him at Athens Airport the previous December he was limping badly. Although the violent atmosphere around the Olympic stadium had not translated into incident, thanks to the high ratio of Greek riot polis to Scots fans, the shit caught up with Lucky later that night. He was taking a midnight stroll in a vain search for a breath of fresh air when he was set upon by a gang of Greeks. Lucky managed to break free and fled into the street where he was hit by a car, leaving him with a broken foot. He had been really looking forward to the trip, with his girlfriend having just packed him in.

The Tartan Army had been warned that Moscow would be a much more threatening place than Athens. Murray had no intention of going midnight strolling alone in this place. In fact he never got the chance to. On arrival at Sheremetyevo 11 airport, Lucky's passport and visa were checked. Through no fault of his own, his visa had not been stamped properly. He was turned around and sent home on the next available plane.

Murray's misfortune reminds me of the passport trouble which John Buchanan and his wife encountered in Munich on their way to the Costa Rica humiliation in 1990. John had recently rescued their joint passport from the jaws of their pet dog. Not too much damage had been done. But inspection by passport control led to their detention by German officials. The dog's dried in saliva, when passed under ultra violet light, made the passport look a forgery. Furthermore, the pair resembled a couple of wanted terrorists.

'I'm not a terrorist. I'm a Hearts fan,' John protested. Some may feel that this is a dubious distinction. Apparently so did the anti-terrorist police as it took several hours of lengthy interrogation before the pair were released.

A lot of the troops travelling to Russia on a tight budget stayed in the Hotel Izmailovo, built for the Olympic Games in 1980, which was located about nine kilometres to the north east of Red Square. The Izmailovo cost $24 a night for a double room. Other hotels, like The Cosmos and the magnificent looking Ukraine, charged a good deal more. The Izmailovo was like no other hotel I'd ever seen. We had been told in advance that it contained 10,000 beds so we were expecting something large. You could see it lit up from miles away. This was more like a high rise housing estate than a hotel. It would not have looked out of place standing in Sighthill in Glasgow, although by now it would probably have been pulled down as a 1960s housing disaster. Four tower blocks

Billets in Moscow: urban blight posing as a hotel.

imaginatively named Block A, Block B, Block C and Block D stood on a characterless concrete concourse broken only by an empty, derelict pool. The fans in the Izmailovo regularly got totally lost on their last leg home. Each block looked exactly the same, with identical wide open foyers, a small bar, a host of large mean looking guys (all carrying 'friends' as the Yanks would term them), the obligatory 'Information' desk where the girl could tell you nothing, a few other stalls and the lift corridor.

After taking the lift, many of the lads stumbled hopelessly along what they were sure was their floor of the hotel, oblivious to the fact that they were in fact billeted a quarter of mile away. The one small clue which helped orientate the lads in one of the blocks was a makeshift sign pinned to the small bar in the foyer. This announced the spot as the 'Giro Bar'. The troops discovered that bottles of vodka could be bought at the nearby market, a collection of shacks planked on a sea of mud, for the equivalent in rubbles of 75p, and that no-one in the Hotel, not least the lady manning the Giro Bar, gave a damn if you brought it in and drank there all night.

There was always Tartan Army posted at the Giro Bar. A common sight from 5 am onwards was the Thompson Twins from Saltcoats. Both wore green tartan British Rail jackets, nicely tailored, that Auld Davie had lent them. The twins resemble slightly younger versions of the wee guy who was always getting slapped about on the Benny Hill Show. Watching them, their similarity was uncanny. They could be speaking to different people, looking in different directions, but their mannerisms, their arm movements, the lot, were perfectly synchronised. Weird. Bob (The Bean) McCreadie was also usually present. The Bean had chucked his job in London a few days before coming to Moscow. On his return he would shortly set off for Australia to see what it was like. No family and no friends there, as yet. But no problem. The Bean didn't think he would make Scotland's next away game in San Marino. He didn't. So things must have gone OK in Oz, for a while anyway. In fact, The Bean did not venture out of the Izmailovo for the duration of his stay in Moscow.

Fife Tartan Army: comrades completely red-nosed in Red Square.

Ladies of the night floated around the foyer and stopped by for a chat at the Giro Bar. In the Izmailovo and in the other hotels the female population would rise between the hours of 4am and 6am. At this time many of the pimps were calling it a night and going home, leaving the girls to make do for themselves. It was a time when prices fell steeply. Many canny Scots turned the period before dawn into a 'Happy Hour' for hookers. Auld Davie's resolve to live a week without entertaining one of his vices crumbled on the last evening. A lassie in black PVC gear who had been pestering a few of the boys at the Giro Bar was to blame.

'Aw, come on then. I'll take ye up tae ma room' proclaimed the auld yin. On arriving on the 23rd floor she apparently demanded 200 dollars. This was not Happy Hour prices. '200 dollars' exclaimed auld Davie. 'I'll gie ye 10 an a'll be looking for change.'

On leaving the tower blocks of the Izmailovo, you had to pass through a little shanty town market to reach the nearest underground station (Izmailovo Park). Some Tartan Army had obviously paused at the shacks to deposit cassette tapes. You could hear Scottish sounds ranging from Jimmy Shand to Gaberlunzie playing through the beat up speakers attached to the top corners of the shacks.

Entering the Moscow underground was an experience. It's a bit like descending into the bowels of the Louvre Museum in Paris. Huge statues, many in martial pose, were everywhere. Carrying guns in public seems to be fashionable in Moscow. For the price of a fraction of a groat you could travel anywhere on the Moscow underground: an ordered and efficient transport system which belied the chaos in the streets above.

Sightseeing is not a priority for many of the footsoldiers. Even so, only a few of the fans failed to step out onto Red Square, pass or enter the black marble mausoleum containing the remains of Lenin, continue on to the marvellously ornate St Basil's Cathedral and return back, past the hawkers of furry hats, dolls and cards of lapel badges and round the corner of the wall of the Kremlin to the spot where the Eternal Flame burns. A magnificent sight to behold in Red Square was the hawkers wandering about wearing *Glagow's Miles Better* tee-shirts and holding up large umbrellas sporting the same message that they themselves had acquired, free of charge, from Tommy Madden, one of Glagow's great Ambassadors and a senior member of the Partick Thistle International Supporters Section. On another occasion a troop of Red Army soldiers was spotted marching across Red Square. Suddenly two Tartan Army joined the group, leading from the front, to make sure the comrades did not get lost.

A small number of fans took organised tours of some description which then left them free to get on with more serious business, like finding Rosie O'Grady's Irish pub. Gordon Smith and Calum Tailor even managed to fix something up before they left home. A guy at Calum's work had a friend in Moscow who was pleased to put them up and give them a tour of the sights. The lady was proud of her city and was really keen to show the boys around. Red Square, the Tomb of the Unknown Soldier and St Basil's. They had virtually done the lot. But by this time Gordon and Calum were famished and could hear Rosie O'Grady's calling. Their Russian host could see that their attention was beginning to turn to drink but she held the trump card till last.

'Friends, would you now like to see the Kremlin. Or would you rather go to McDonalds?' The poor lady was now emotionally exposed. 'Lets go to McDonalds' they replied together. Gordon remembers her look of utter devastation. But at least the lassie was beginning to understand the Tartan Army. An army can't march on culture alone.

Standing back from it all, I suspect that more sightseeing of a traditional kind was done in Moscow than in many other places we've been. Certainly in Rome, where we were defeated 3:1 by Italy in 1993, the neglect shown by the Tartan Army of the architectural and historical culture of that once great imperial city could be construed as verging on the criminal.

There is not much to say about McDonalds in Moscow except that it was busier than most McDonalds we'd been in. From there, many fans made their way to Rosie O'Grady's, a walk of about 15 minutes. Rosie's was also jumpin'. There we met a few Scots, Irish and English who were working in Moscow, often in the building trade over which the Irish, we were told, enjoyed a fair amount of control. Early in the week an Irish fella approached Paddy McLaughlin and asked if Wee Murray the Piper could turn up at a surprise going away do for a Scots lad he was organising on the Thursday evening.

'No problem,' said Paddy and took down the address.

On the Monday a character who was soon to take on a legendary status among the Tartan Army appeared in Rosie's. He introduced himself as Jacko and announced that all Scotland fans should accompany him at once to the Casino Moscow on the ground floor of the Hotel Leningradskaya. There we would find free drink, dancing girls and music for as long as we could stand.

The boys who were there at the time thought to themselves 'We've only been in this city for a day or so at the most. There's got to be a catch here somewhere.' But they went and there wasn't. What they found could be found all week in Jacko's. Tartan Army everywhere. Dancing on the tables and the bar, rock music blaring, the Tartan Army singing along to *We still haven't found what we're looking for*, wall to wall strippers, the lot. Jacko's place was bouncing for the best part of a week. At any one time there could be up to 200 Scots in complete heaven.

David Jackson, or Jacko, originally hails from Hamilton, although he's been working casinos all round the world for around two decades. He was working in Iran when the Shah was overthrown. Jacko set up and managed Casino Moscow, the city's first, but now one of many. Knowing that Scotland were soon to be playing in Moscow, Jacko had faxed the SFA in advance, inviting the players and officials to his casino to enjoy his hospitality. The offer was declined by return fax. Once the team and officials arrived in Moscow, Jacko went to their hotel seeking an audience with Mr Jim Farry, Chief Executive of the SFA. He said he could tell from several paces that his personal approach would not work, so he about turned and left without discussion.

News of Jacko's place spread gradually among the Tartan Army. Sadly some folk, to their eternal regret, never made it along. I first heard about the place late Tuesday morning from Davie Pollock when we were relaxing in Rosie's. Davie had been there on the Monday and began recounting the scenes he had witnessed. Then someone announced that Jacko had been stabbed and rushed to hospital earlier that morning. It had been a nasty one. Jacko had been ushering a Russian towards the entrance. Things looked like they were going smoothly when at the last moment the Russian turned and lunged at Jacko with a knife. Jacko saw it coming and managed to deflect the blade, but it still left a gash in his chest which required 15 stitches.

At the time Jacko had been wearing a Scotland football top given to him earlier in the evening by Neil Aitken (a Rod Stewart look-alike) from Coldstream. As his Saltire announces around the world, Neil is a 'Glazier and Joiner.' At the hospital the Scotland top was removed to allow treatment. Then it was removed altogether, apparently stolen by one of the doctors. Neil was very distressed when he later found out that someone had slashed his shirt. But more importantly, Jacko survived and made the under 21 game later that day, which is more than can be said for a sizeable number of the Tartan Army.

One thing that has to be said about Jacko is that he has marvellous style. An irrepressible personality and a gifted master of ceremonies. It would be impossible to remain in a catatonic state with Jacko leading the proceedings. The show he put on for the troops was out of this world. In fact Jacko's life in Moscow was featured in a double page spread in the *Sunday Mail* on 9 April under the title *Life on the Wild Side*. A reporter had travelled out to see Jacko after tales had filtered back home. He wrote about how lucrative, but dangerous, casino life in Moscow was. The reporter cited a young Australian couple who had started work as croupiers but lasted less than a week after several hold ups and attacks by gangsters. Risky perhaps, but it certainly seemed to be lucrative. One of the croupiers we were drinking with, a half English - half Italian lad called Vince, was clearing four to five grand a week.

The reporter from the *Sunday Mail* also talked about the dangers of taking a taxi late at night. He warned that what would seem like a cab would stop, you'd get in, then you'd get robbed and pushed out, if you were lucky. Good advice for tourists perhaps, but there was little chance of any Tartan Army in the know relying on taxis in Moscow. Every car was a taxi. All you need to do is stick out your hand and the first passing Lada with a cracked windscreen would pull over. You would then do a deal with the driver in dollars and away you'd go. All Ladas in Moscow have broken

Wee Murray piping his heart out in Rosie O'Grady's.

windows it seems. A new, intact windscreen has a short life expectancy, in the owner's car at least. It is very likely to be whipped out and sold on. Hence, one of the first things the new car owner does is to hit the windscreen, crack it and improve his chances of keeping it.

The Lada technique was the one we used late on Thursday afternoon to get ourselves from Rosie O'Grady's to where wee

Murray had promised a surprise piping performance. Five of us arrived at what looked like an office building with no sign of life inside. However, a push on the glass door and it swung open. Up the stairs and we found the Irishman who had requested Murray's appearance. He was delighted and gave instructions as to precisely when Murray should appear. This came after a fine presentation speech celebrating the time the Scots chap had spent with his company in Moscow. Over the course of the speech several presents were handed over, the last being a large, antique volume of Robert Louis Stevenson's book *Kidnapped*. Then it was upstairs to another floor for a splendid buffet and bevvy. It can be a mistake to speak to too many Russians at these occasions. Every new hand you shake presses a glass of cold vodka into yours and great offence is taken if the vodka is not downed in one gulp.

From the reception it was back to the Hotel Ukraine to drop off wee Murray and his mother Cathy. The Hotel Ukraine at night reminds you of the buildings in the centre of Gotham City, the sinister urban setting of the *Batman* comics and movies. There are close parallels between Gotham City and Moscow. Both are deeply threatening places and characterised by chaos and runaway crime. But one is the stuff of fiction, the other is very, very real. By the end of the campaign many of the footsoldiers were talking about leaving 'Gotham City,' not Moscow.

A casual observer during the Moscow campaign might well have spotted a strange sight moving among groups of Scots - a thin, pale faced lad with a top, knitted tammie and scarf all in the colours of Liverpool. His name was Dimitri and a group of us had literally bumped into him as we rounded a corner on our way along deserted side streets from McDonalds to find Rosie O'Grady's on the Sunday. He had once been to Merseyside and didn't want to let go of the memory. He spent the next four days hanging out with the fans, helping now and again with little details like how to find the Bar Sport, an underground station, and so on. But those who took time for a blether with him were astounded by his encyclopedic knowledge of English football; old teams, players, games and scores. This was obviously his life. He was treated kindly.

On match day about fourteen of us poured into two 'taxis' hailed down near the Izmailovo to head for Jacko's. Mad Dog McLeod and Chiz were now in tow. They had arrived on the Tuesday after the marathon train journey from Tallinn. Jacko's was buzzing from noon with well over a hundred fans packed in for over six hours of revelry. Saltires, naked ladies, rampant lions, flailing bodies, sweat, noise and lots of bevvy. A few troops peeled themselves away late afternoon to make their way to the stadium, but the great majority partied on. About 6pm Jacko announced that a couple of coaches would be outside to take the remaining troops to the game. It needed a human shoe horn to pack us in and we were off.

The game against Russia was played in the Luzhniki Stadium which had hosted the Olympic Games in 1980. The place had deteriorated a bit since then. One of the fans complained about getting a skelf deeply embedded in the cheek of his arse. The police presence in and around the stadium was pretty heavy and totally humourless. Reports later filtered back that a coach load of fans, for no apparent reason, had been turned away from the ground. On my own way in I stopped to talk to a group of about twenty Russian skinheads dressed in black gear and heavy boots. I offered them some popcorn but they didn't seem to have an appetite. Their leader-off could speak pretty good English. We chatted for a few minutes but I couldn't figure out what was really going through his mind. I think he was a little bemused as these men in skirts and other regalia swept by to the skirl of the pipes. He seemed a nice lad and it would have been pleasant to spend a little longer blethering.

In the stadium the Tartan Army was stationed looking down onto the stretch of track which Alan Wells had blasted

Tartan Army entertains the Red Army.

Jacko's Banquet: free food, free drink; the hospitality was endless at The Casino Moscow.

along to lift gold for Scotland in the 100 meters Olympics back in 1980. It put a lump in my throat to think back to that night. Wells, single minded, superbly conditioned and bursting with power, sank into his blocks and held his concentration depite the nasal problems of the Cuban to his left. But the main threat came from further away, in lane one, in the shape of another Cuban, Silvio Leonard. Wells kept his focus. The gun cracked and the rest is history.

Scotland's footballers could not possibly have covered themselves in the glory that Alan Wells did almost 15 years earlier, but they played with concentration and great commitment. They also carried a wee bit of luck, for a change. Scotland walked off with a point after a 0:0 draw as a paraglider circled high above the pitch.

There was a lovely, moving moment back at Jacko's a few hours after the game. Jacko took the mike and interrupted the mayhem.

'Right lads, I want you all to follow me. There is food coming in ten minutes.' About one hundred and sixty of us then filed through the Casino and into a huge banqueting hall with places all laid out. 'Before the food arrives, there will be one minute silence for Davie Cooper.' Davie, whose legendary status among the Tartan Army was secured by his late penalty equaliser against Wales which sent Scotland to the Mexico World Cup in 1986, had died suddenly just days before the fans had left for Russia. You could have heard a pin drop as everyone stood at their places.

The physically exhausted Tartan Army broke up in Moscow and started to make their various ways home. That is with the exception of Kevin Lewis from Burntisland, who made his way down through Eastern Europe and met up with everyone again at the next game in San Marino. Kevin's travels were not without incident, which included a mugging in Prague followed up by two weeks recuperating in the company of a delightful local Czech girl.

For the returning fans, coming back direct by plane was the least painless, although airport bureaucracy has an especially cruel face when you haven't slept for three days and your goodwill is fraying about the edges. But for the lads taking the long train journey back to Tallinn, airport queues would have been a luxury. When they had initially bought their train tickets in Tallinn, some of the troops had paid less for the return leg than the outward journey. They couldn't understand this at the time, but they soon found out. They were travelling back third class. A total nightmare. It gave them some idea what it would have been like to be transported to the saltmines in Outer Siberia and a few developed a new found sympathy for the plight of veal calves in transit which was receiving considerable press coverage at the time.

Despite the occasional hardships, one of the advantages of overland travel is that, even on tired return legs, small incidents happen that stick in the mind. Here's Wee Geordie again, one of the train travellers, with an incident from the journey back:

> Two Tartan Army members returning from Moscow disembarked from the Tallinn hydrofoil in Helsinki. They had an afternoon to kill in the expensive capital before they caught their flight home. With their last £20 it was decided they visit the bar in the railway station for a pint and a spin on the roulette table to see if they could get drunk on luck.
>
> Accompanying them was the ex-Estonian football team manager (who was in charge of the side for Scotland's game with them in May 1993). He had introduced himself to them on the hydrofoil – resplendent in an SFA tie (a present from Mr James Farry).
>
> The lads needed to keep £10 to pay for the bus journey from the city centre to the airport – a distance of about 6 miles. After a couple of pints and a heavy losing streak they soon had no money left and were down to their last chip. Faced with a gruelling journey to catch their now impending flight (check-in time was less than 2 hours away) it was decided they would put their faith in one of the most famous of Scots heroes, Robert the

Bruce. With their last chip they played a cheval in-between the numbers 13/14. The wheel was spun, the ball rolled and the 2 pals looked away in apprehension. Then with an ecstatic squeal the lady croupier announced 'red thirteen…' and with a triumphant (but relieved) shout the footsoldiers collected their winnings and got another pint before boarding the airport bus followed by their flight home.

Surely now everyone must believe the Good Lord is a Scotsman!

Billy Dunn, the famous late returner, was in action again on the way back from Moscow. Billy, a fisherman from Pittenweem, is a serial passport loser. He carries one of the shiny red passports, much like the ten year version that most of us now have. But Billy's is specially stamped by the Passport Office 'valid for one year only,' the authorities' response to his repeated loss of British passports on foreign soil over many years. In fact, on one occasion in Sweden in 1995, Billy was in the process of reporting the loss of a 'one year' passport. The official, after taking his details, returned somewhat confused.

'You are Mr William Dunn from Pittenweem? Mr Dunn, this is all very strange. We do have a passport here for you. But it is a ten year passport which we have had since 1992.'

'Is it still valid?,' enquired Billy. It was. 'That'll do fine then.'

On the Moscow trip, Billy had been one of the train party, travelling with Russell Ritchie and staying at the Izmailovo Hotel. Russell ordered two taxis to get the immediate group across the city to the train station. He thought Billy was in the second taxi. He wasn't. Billy was still back at the Izmailovo.

His pals discovered their loss when they saw the contents of the other taxi empty without producing anyone that looked remotely like Billy. Billy discovered that he was left behind (again) when he strolled into the Hotel bar and found himself alone except for the gun-toting, plain clothes characters who are a permanent feature of the residence. Meanwhile back at the station, the troops had no time to return to pick up Billy. But they felt they had to do something to help their stranded pal when they realised they had his passport and visa. Luckily there was the customary lady in tow to kiss goodbye to a new found loved one.

And there were quite a few of these situations: like those involving Jim Black who returned to Moscow one month later to visit Jacko's bar and a girl he met there; or a lad from Cumbernauld (Andrew Gray) who married his Russian sweetheart over a year later.

So the troops beseeched the lady to return to the Izmailovo, find Billy Dunn and hand over the essential travel documents and a bundle of cash they had mustered between them. These were duly delivered to Billy who then discovered another problem. He had Ally Benton's air ticket. Ally (who with fellow footsoldier Stevie Geddes hails from Stonehaven) was not part of the train group, but somehow he'd got his and Billy's tickets mixed up. And Ally had left for the airport earlier that day. He only noticed the problem at the check-in, but it didn't seem to bother the Russian at the desk.

Billy Dunn did, eventually, get out of Russia after a payment of $30 for a ticket upgrade, or more likely a bribe. In any case, Billy got home before the train travellers who were a couple of days behind him. Billy Dunn getting home early? A real one off.

Moscow was tough on the body and quite a few of us came back in bits. At least it felt like that. Danny Divers, who had enjoyed three hours sleep in seventy two hours went straight to work behind the bar of the Captain's Cabin pub he managed, at that time, in Newbury. Drying glasses after closing time he felt the heat spread from his stomach to his neck. Danny was convinced he was having a heart attack. He hadn't been near a doctor for over ten years, but in a panic phoned himself an ambulance. As he was receiving treatment in the back of the vehicle he started to tell the crew stories about Moscow, about Jacko's and about what he'd been up to for the last three days. Any sympathy the medical staff had for their patient quickly evaporated and Danny, who was merely experiencing early withdrawal symptoms, was dumped onto the pavement by the paramedics who had better things to do.

Another returning traveller also thought he was breathing his last on the flight home. He had also been enjoying Jacko's hospitality for several days and had spent his final few hours in the

Izmailovo consuming Vodka of a quality which any self respecting street drunk would have turned their nose up at. High in the sky, as Wee Murray played the pipes for the passengers, this bloke was lying in a seriously bad way in the aisle. The stewardesses were alarmed. As one tried to comfort the sweating wretch another scanned the passenger list. They were lucky, there was a doctor on the flight. On the tannoy she could just be heard above the skirl of the pipes,

'Can Dr. McArthur please come to the front of the front of the plane, we have a passenger in urgent need of assistance.' Meanwhile the ailing one was struggling to attract the speaker's attention - arms pawing as he could barely speak.

The stewardess bent down, 'Please relax' she reassured him, 'everything will be OK. Help is on its way.'

'No, no, you don't understand,' he gasped, 'I'm Dr. McArthur.'

On return from Moscow the Tartan Army discovered that they had missed a TV event of colossal proportions. The BBC had conspired to screen a show of *This is Your Life* featuring Jimmy Hill while hundreds of people who have shown a great interest in Mr Hill over the years were thousands of miles away. He was, of course, not forgotten while we were in Moscow. In Jacko's, one Scot was dancing away, stripped to the waist, with the Jimmy Hill song painted on his body in waterproof mascara, in Russian, courtesy of a local hooker. In the background, a makeshift banner announced the famous anthem in full in the same language. A story also filtered back that a couple of fans who had travelled to the outlying country of Uzbekistan came across a pub where the locals were singing about Mr Hill in their native tongue and had tried to teach the Scots the words. It seems that people wish to sing about Jimmy Hill in many different languages.

But the final word on the Russian campaign must be about Jacko. The great man was still showing hospitality to Scots when Jim Black returned to say hello to a Russian girlfriend a month later. And he was still there in June when Jim and Kenny (The General) Reid (so called because of the Soviet army medals, bought in a Tallinn flea market, that he wears on the breast of his pipers jacket) placed a telephone call to his casino from a latchkey club in Torshaven in the Faroe Islands run by a guy from Maryhill. But sad news, for Scots visiting Moscow, found its way to Craig McDowall of the London Scottish a year after our visit in the form of an email message. A certain John Cairns had been surfing the Net and had come across the Tartan Army Home Page. His email to Craig on 27 March, 1997 read as follows:

> I have just finished flicking through some pages of your club and was happy to see the story relating to your visit to Moscow for the game here in Russia. I still do not think the locals here have got over the sights and sounds.
>
> With regard to the main man, Jacko, I will try and give you an update. There are many different stories as to what happened to Jacko. You may have seen him appear as himself in the film *Police Academy 7* (in Moscow). One rumour has it that he went to Hollywood to further his acting career though there are many others. He has become more popular than Elvis here with sightings of him in Puerto Rico, Rio De Janeiro, Bangkok, Phuket as well as many less well known destinations.
>
> Jacko disappeared last year, just around the time the tax police, Mafia and the owners of the casino moved in, although it was difficult to know who was who. There was a lot of talk at the time as to what Jacko had taken with him. But one of the things he definitely took was his kindness, humour and generosity, especially if you were a fellow Scot. He is sadly missed by everyone who had the pleasure of knowing him.

Jim Black with Jacko (2nd from left) last seen contemplating a career in Russian politics.

Since Jacko left the place has never been the same. Everybody stopped going there, the casino was closed down and the bar was empty and even the band left.

Should there be any future sightings, I will let you know the country and establishment, just in case there is any of you who will be going to that part of the world.

CHAPTER 3

SAVE THE WHALE

THE FAROE ISLANDS ARE a remote and beautiful place. The kind of fixture that the Tartan Army relishes. I recall the cheer in the Bruce Tavern in Dunfermline that greeted the addition of the Faroe Islands to Scotland's qualifying section for the 1996 European Championship when the draw was made early 1994. Do go to the Faroes if you get a chance. But whatever you do, don't slag off pilot whaling. And if you do choose to criticise the long standing practice of whale slaughter, then be prepared for a beautiful place to become very unwelcoming indeed. This was certainly the message put over by a TV documentary on the plight of pilot whales which was shown on TV a couple of weeks before the Tartan Army set sail for the Scotland game in June 1995.

The programme was real horror movie material. Since 1856, when the Danish trade monopoly over the Faroes was abolished (the Islands having been under the Danish Crown since 1380), a sizeable fleet of fishing vessels has provided the population with its main industry and source of income. These boats kill a lot of whales. The documentary showed Faroese boats of all sizes herding a large team, or pod, of pilot whales into a small bay. There can be hundreds of whales in a pod and they all bunch together, following the leader. Under the circumstances this is an instinctively tactical mistake. For once into the shallows of the bay, they are gaffed and butchered: a carnage which sees the ocean turn red as the mammals thrash about in their death throes. The gory spectacle is a community event. Able bodied men lean from the boats and saw away, cutting deep into the back of the animals' necks. Others help haul the dead and dying whales ashore while the rest of the community watch from a short distance away. Only the very young and the infirm do not take part.

In years gone by the culling of whales was essential for community survival. The meat was shared freely among the population and the rest of the carcasses were also put to good use. Nothing was wasted. Many argue that this is no longer the case and point to the substantial remains of whales which are left to rot on the beaches. Environmentalists froth at the mouth when faced with a custom which they see as threatening the survival of a beautiful species. The documentary found only a few local people who were critical of whaling, but none that would appear on camera. The interviewers reported considerable hostility towards themselves as they went about their investigations. The Faroese are very touchy about their whales and visitors to their islands would do well to heed these sensitivities.

It should be said that the timing of the programme was purely coincidental. There was no suggestion that the investigative journalists were particularly concerned with the welfare of Scotland's travelling support. But advance intelligence, intended or not, can be useful for an army preparing to march, or sail. It gave a few of the Tartan Army time to purchase inflatable dolphins – the nearest thing that could readily be obtained from toy shops which bore a very close resemblance to a pilot whale. The dolphins were duly inflated, decked out with tartan scarves and tammies and carried shoulder high as the great bulk of the travelling support disembarked from the *Smyril* to set foot on terra firma for the first time in 24 hours. This was Torshaven, the main town, in the Faroes. A substantial proportion of the population was at the quayside to greet their visitors who returned the welcome with resounding chorus of:

Save the Whale
Save the Whale
We're the Famous Tartan Army
And we're here to Save the Whale

The Faroese took it all in good humour and the Tartan Army, just to show that we were not there to take sides in the environmental debate about marine conservation, searched the few fast food outlets trading in Torshaven in vain for pilot whale burgers and chips. This, according to the TV documentary, would have been at some risk to the supporters' health. The programme had concluded with a comment that due to the dumping of toxic waste in the ocean, the meat from pilot whales is contaminated by mercury. In this tragic way the whales are getting their own back.

The *Smyril* was a friendly ship. The crew were relaxed and the hospitality was warm. It was a warmth which continued throughout the whole trip. While some fans took advantage of the kitchen's relaxed approach to catering to prepare grub for the masses, others spent time up on the bridge assisting the captain and his fellow officers. He displayed charts of our route and of the Faroe Islands, eighteen of them in all, and the troops took turns at the big wheel. The vessel was probably on a set course, but the weans enjoyed kidding on they were steering it all the same. The *Smyril's* transportation of the Tartan Army was the first time the ship had carried such a sizeable contingent of football fans. Sadly, it was also the last. More than a few Scottish fans were disappointed to hear the news that the direct service between Aberdeen and Torshaven was to be stopped in 1997.

The seaborne invasion of the Faroes lasted a week in all. The *Smyril* left Aberdeen on the Sunday afternoon and returned the following Saturday around mid-day. A lot of the troops travelled

as 'deck' passengers. This meant you didn't have a cabin, but there were large luggage racks on the top deck which served marvellously as makeshift bunks where you could dump your gear and crash out. Booking independently, deck travel cost £110 for

On the luggage deck of the Smyril:
no bunks, just luxury luggage racks to sleep in.

the return passage: a pretty good deal. But for only a few pounds more you could have had a cabin. Those travelling with Grigor enjoyed this extra bit of luxury.

Some folk chose to fly, mostly via Copenhagen. Indeed, this was the mode and route of travel which Tam (Four Fingers) Ritchie elected to use. Johnny Marr and some other regular campaigners had met Tam for the first time a few weeks earlier in San Marino, but the Faroes was to be my first exposure to this deformed comedian who readers will get to know well in later chapters of the book. Other airborne troops came with a commercial football travel operator (which we will call *Fawlty Tours*). This company offered a fly-direct package, the cost of which was close to £400. Flying out on the morning of the game and returning the next day wouldn't give the *Fawlty Tours* travellers much chance to relax and get to know the Faroes. As it turned out they got a lot less than they expected.

Things started to go wrong with the *Fawlty Tours* trip from the outset. Instead of flying straight from Glasgow on the Wednesday morning, I understand they were bussed to Aberdeen, then flown to Wick. At Wick they were forced to change planes. The new plane had a problem with weight and the fans had to shed some. The weight loss came painfully in the form of the carryouts. They were not permitted to be taken on board. And worse was to come. No alcohol was sold on the flight. A Gobi Desert in the air. But *Fawlty Tours* got them there, eventually. The travellers arrived at the game 23 minutes after kick off.

There was considerable sympathy for the *Fawlty Tours* group when news got around of the hassles they had faced. Someone made the sensible suggestion that having paid £400 and having missed one third of the game they should demand a hefty refund.

'Nonsense,' declared one dissenting voice. 'They should have been charged more than £400. They didn't have to suffer the whole ninety minutes.'

One guy fared even worse than the *Fawlty Tours* fans, or better depending on your point of view. This fella flew to Copenhagen, then to Iceland and from there sailed to the Faroes. He arrived on Tuesday the day before the game, and was in fine fettle for a few hours. Unfortunately, he was soon to discover that he'd only the Tuesday night to enjoy. A close inspection of the connection times for his return journey revealed that in order to make his Iceland-Denmark flight he had to return to Iceland the following morning – the morning of the game! Hopefully he got a chance to hear the game on the radio on the boat back.

Limited transportation options, and two away games against Russia and San Marino in the previous couple of months, led to a fairly modest turnout by Tartan Army standards. But these kind of campaigns, where you find yourselves all together in a small remote part of the world, often turn out to be the best. I heard that someone had phoned the Faroes Tourist Office after the draw and found that the office staff were already in the midst of a party celebrating the coming visit of Scotland.

One local friendship had already been forged. This occurred a few months earlier in Athens, prior to Scotland's qualifying game for the Euro '96 Championships against Greece; a disappointing 1:0 defeat. (Lisbon) Liz Denholm and her friend Felice had just dumped their gear at the hotel and were on their way to join a party of Tartan Army already well into the pre-match celebrations in the Hotel Stanley. As they were leaving they bumped into the guy from the room next door.

'He looked like a wee window cleaner who had hit hard times,' recalls Lisbon Liz. The girls invited him to join them for a drink. 'We are here for a football match against Greece,' Liz explained in the taxi, 'it is the first time the two countries have ever played each other.'

'And how are Scotland performing?' the window cleaner asked.

'Not bad,' replied Liz. 'We got off to a good start beating Finland 2:0 away from home and then

Lisbon Liz - and a very auld flame!

hammered five past a team called the Faroe Islands. But they were complete shite and still even managed to score one against us. Then we held Russia to a draw in Moscow.'

'And do you like football?' she asked.

'Yes, I like football very much,' he said.

Lisbon Liz and Felice couldn't understand what was going on when they arrived at the Hotel Stanley. The Tartan Army were queuing up to shake this guy's hand and buy him drink. The window cleaner turned out to be Alan Simonsen, the great Danish international, capped over 50 times by his country, a former European Player of the Year and scorer of a winning penalty against England at Wembley. Also, he was (and at the time of writing, still is) the manager of the Faroe Islands and was in Athens to observe two of his team's future opponents. Alan gave the girls his telephone number and told them they were welcome to get in touch if they were coming to the Faroes next June.

The affection the Faroese have for the Scots possibly dates from the Second World War when the Islands were occupied by British forces while the rest of the Danish Kingdom was under the Nazi jackboot. Apparently the Faroese fishermen performed heroics to supply Scotland with 20 per cent of the fish we needed during the War years, and 132 of them died doing it.

The great Alan Simonson – mistaken for a window cleaner.

Motherwell F.C. had given Faroese-Scots relations a more recent boost during a European Cup tie. The 'Well fans left a good impression and a few maroon and yellow scarves around the necks of local kids. But we like to think the locals had also heard of the Famous Tartan Army and were anticipating a boisterous and colourful week that would boost the flagging local economy.

The Faroe Islands, which lie halfway between Iceland and the Shetlands, have a population of 44,500. First impressions are of a fairly prosperous wee place. Torshaven, with its population of 15,000 and a backdrop of snow capped hills, was delightful and spotlessly clean. But according to some of the locals we spoke to, things were not going too well. Taxes are high and the islands are heavily dependent on subsidy from the Danish government. One lad told us that the population was falling steadily and that young people just wanted to get away as there was little future for them on the islands.

The Tartan Army was certainly struck by the lack of young people, or more precisely young lassies, in the vicinity of Torshaven. There was a worrying gap in the age profile of the population. Between schools kids under 16 years old and married women with kids, the female population was very thin on the ground. It brought to mind the film *The Magnificent Seven.* Remember when Yul Brynner and his troops arrived in this wee Mexican town to help ward off the bad guys (led by Eli Wallach) and found only adult men. The women and the weans had been spirited away and hidden in the safety of the forest. I doubt the Faroese really suspected the Tartan Army was hell bent on rape and pillage though the behaviour of a few footsoldiers got pretty close to it. Many of the the young folk were away to Denmark for their education or in search of work.

The houses, mostly built of wood and many with turf roofs, were painted in a variety of bright colours. I guess it's important to do all you can with a few licks of paint to keep the spirits of the population up in a part of the world which is in round-the-clock darkness during the depths of winter. We were, fortunately, catching the place at its best, in June when the daylight lasts for 24 hours. This may sound idyllic, and it was. But it can have its downside. The absence of night, or more accurately daybreak, gives the reveller no help in deciding when to hit the kip. Perfect conditions for the Tartan Army!

But despite these optimal seasonal conditions, a week-long campaign will require some footsoldiers to slip in some slumber. And on these occasions the turf roofs came in very handy. It was a common sight, when stoatin' along the road in the wee small hours, to look up and see a kilted contingent sleeping peacefully on someone's grass roof with a couple of crates of beer from the local brewery at arms reach.

Apart from the odd roof here and there the fans were billeted around a number of apartments, bed and breakfasts and the Torshaven Youth Hostel. The Youth Hostel, located about a mile up the hill from the town, was a fairly basic affair: a sizeable canteen area with tables and chairs and a small kitchen off it and what looked like a sports hall which had been sectioned up with makeshift partitions to create small cubicles each containing two double bunks. A few of the Tartan Army had reserved accommodation at the Hostel as part of Ian Sharp's party, others just turned up and stationed

Torshaven Youth Hostel, The Faroes: a liquor-free zone, apparently.

themselves there. The other guests who were there to hillwalk or bird watch must have felt they had arrived in the 'Youth Hostel from Hell.' The canteen housed an almost continuous party for the whole week.

Word soon got around about where it was all happening. Towards the end of the week locals in the only night club in Torshaven, Club 20, invited a team of Scots to a party when the Club shut at midnight. The Scots fans, believing they had cracked a house party, jumped into cars only to find themselves being driven up to the Youth Hostel where they were already staying.

Yes, there were some queer sights in and around that Hostel. One evening a young Faroese lad became so distressed after seeing his girlfriend disappear into the darkness of the dormitory hall with a Scot that he ran outside, cut his wrists and proceeded to bang his head repeatedly off a jeep. Thankfully there were few unsavoury incidents like this and most of the Faroese proved to be very easy going people indeed. On the Thursday evening, Pickle,

Mad Dog and Mad Harry, while making their way back to barracks engaged the company of a horse which had been passing time in a nearby field. The farmer, who owned the horse, must have been a light sleeper and chased the trio up the road. The animal was successfully retrieved a couple of hundred yards from the Hostel.

Harry later returned and took the farmer's cow. This time it was Ian Sharp, sober, and in a position of some responsibility having arranged a block booking at the Youth Hostel, who spied Mad Harry and his guest arriving. Ian returned the cow and was really pissed off when he arrived back at the Hostel forty minutes later.

'Could he not have picked a closer farm? The cow belongs to the place at the bottom of the hill' he moaned.

The group of raiders was enlarged with the addition of Johnny Marr, Joker of the London Scottish and Tam Scones (from Scone) for one last crack at enhancing the interior decoration of the Youth Hostel. This time the target was an inanimate object in the shape of a set of goal posts, full size with nets, which they removed from a nearby football training ground. But it was not third time lucky. On this occasion they were foiled by the Hostel itself as it proved impossible to manoeuvre the goals through the inner doors of the building.

Housing the Tartan Army is not a stress free challenge. Wee Geordie recalls a conversation with the Hostel warden on the last night of the occupation. The warden manned a small room with a window overseeing the whole canteen area. At the side of the window a large sign announced that 'It is strictly forbidden to bring alcohol into the Hostel.' You could just see the top of the letters appearing above stacked empty crates of the local brew, *Gull Export Beer*. The warden's name was Thomas. He had just started in the job the previous Sunday, the day the fans arrived. By Thursday night Thomas was physically and emotionally drained: white as a sheet with eyes like dug's baws. The poor lad told Geordie he couldn't handle it and was going to hand in his notice. This was after only four days in the job.

Supermarket trolleys were in and out of the Youth Hostel. A number of these had been requisitioned from the local supermarket and performed a vital function in beer transportation, shifting empty crates of Gull Export back to the brewery and returning with full ones. In fact these trolleys worked all over Torshaven. Local residents looked on curiously as the trolley traffic moved up and down the main street during working hours. Empty crates stacked several high on trolleys were pushed up the hill passing fully laden trolleys descending from the brewery and restrained with firm grips to minimise the horrible prospect of a 'runaway cairy oot.'

As they stared at themselves in the mirror of the local hairdressers, Johnny Marr and Gudge could see the trolleys passing by in the street behind them. But the girls in the salon seemed fully preoccupied with the job at hand. The boys had thrown them a bit by asking for a style of cut they had not delivered before.

'Look, if yi've got a bit of paper and a pen and I'll draw ye what we're after,' offered Gudge. He drew a Saltire. The stylists got the message and proceeded to give the backs of both heads a close crop before cutting two outlines of the St Andrew's Cross.

On the morning of the match a group of fans leaving the Hostel paused at the nearby football ground to watch some of the Scotland squad go through a light training session. The fans were a colourful assembly. Along with the tartan regalia they sported a collection of gear much of which had been acquired on previous campaigns. This included a Russian tank commander's hat, Estonian naval uniforms, a kaftan, Russian military jackets, a Russian Mig fighter pilot's helmet, and two stuffed puffins purchased in the Faroes and perched on the shoulder epaulets of Mad Dog's and Gudge's piper jackets. The puffins remained there for the duration of the campaign and have seen active service since.

Alex McLeish, who was knocking high balls in for keeper Nicky Walker, smiled and shouted over, 'Listen lads, we'll be finished in a few minutes. Wait there. There's plenty of balls here. We'll take some pot shots and knock you down.'

'Have a go then, but you could knock us down with a feather' laughed one of the spectators.

'What?' exclaimed Mad Dog, 'to hell with that. If we were to wait for you lot to knock us down we'd be here all day. I'm away for a beer.'

There weren't many indoor places to imbibe in Torshaven. The closest thing resembling a pub was a small establishment called Café Nature. It was not cheap. A small beer came in at around the equivalent of £6. Faced with prices like these the attraction of the brewery off-licence, where bottles of Gull Export could be had for £1, was understandable. Still the atmosphere in Café Nature was good. As usual, the music system was taken over by *the Corries* and other tapes pre-prepared for the campaign.

For a couple of days Sheila was the centre of attention in the Nature. Sheila was a sheep who had been liberated from the local supermarket. Independent movement for Sheila was difficult. The animal had no legs or body, just a head, and a skinned one at that. Otherwise she was the picture of health, with lovely eyes and fine set of teeth. During her two day spell with the Tartan Army, Sheila did it all. She drank, smoked and even had her teeth cleaned by Tam Scoons. Tam didn't have his own toothbrush and toothpaste with him at the time, but there were plenty of alternatives handy as some of the troops had dumped their bags in the Nature for the week.

Sheila also made the game, although the look on the steward's face as her match brief was handed over suggested that her benefactor could have saved himself a few bob. She would have got in without a ticket. No doubt she recognised some of the players from her earlier visit to the players' hotel. The timing of this visit was slightly unfortunate as the players and staff were in the midst of their evening meal. But Sheila insisted. Big Alex McLeish also insisted in finding out what was in the polly bag the fan was carrying.

'It's Sheila, the sheep's head' he was informed.

'Aye that'll be right. What's really in it?' Big Alex didn't look too interested in his dinner after he met Sheila.

Sheila was enjoying herself, but there was no denying it, she was past her sell by date. Her final two days had been full and eventful and she bowed out in style. Around one o'clock in the morning after the game Sheila was boiled in the kitchen of the Youth Hostel to make a large pot of soup. Other, less wholesome, ingredients also found their way into this brew. I'm sure I saw at least one Brillo pad swirling around as Four Fingers ladled out helpings to a few unfortunate footsoldiers as well as some grateful looking Norwegians who had just arrived from a few days birdwatching in the mountains.

Another indoor haunt discovered during the week was the Mimir. Founded in 1967, it is one of the oldest 'Keyclubs' in the Faroe Islands. On payment of a 100kr deposit and 50kr for membership you are normally given your own key to come and go when the club is open in the evenings. You would never know it was there. It looked just like an ordinary house. But someone stumbled into it and passed the word. No deposits or membership fees were requested from the Scots fans. A knock at the door found a warm welcome from the manager, a Glaswegian called Terry who had been in the Faroes for close to 20 years. It was difficult for the fans to buy a drink in the Mimir as we first had to drink our way through several crates of beer which Terry put on the house.

To get to the match many of us took to the sea again, a forty minute sail from Torshaven on the island of Streymoy to the tiny settlement of Toftir on the island of Eysturoy. A bid had been made on the Wednesday afternoon to hire a helicopter. Myself and Four Fingers had reached an advanced stage in negotiations with a charming lady in the Torshaven Tourist Office.

The helicopter could carry a dozen. It would be a five minute flight at a cost of around £30 per minute. And no, the lady did not think it was out of the question for the helicopter to land us on the park. Things looked good until she tried to finalise the details over the phone.

Her expression had saddened by the time she put down the receiver and said 'I am very sorry, but the helicopter is broken. It will not be ready to fly for two days.'

Landing at the Toftir stadium in the helicopter would have been spectacular. The pitch is located at the top of the hill which rises steeply from the sea. The fans wound their way up the small road which twists up the hillside or scrambled a more direct route over rough grass and boulders. Security going into the ground was leaky, and fans without briefs found no difficulty getting in simply by walking backwards past the stewards who were collecting tickets.

Before the kick off there was a presentation to David McLaren, the SFA's Chief Security Advisor and a real nice guy, who was retiring after the Faroes. The lovely Marjory Nimmo, who runs the SFA Travel Club, had passed a farewell card for signing among the fans over the previous couple of days. It's likely that Mr McLaren would have had some difficulty reading all the goodwill messages, as even the fans who wrote them probably would. And

Sorry Mr McLaren. (And thanks from the Tartan Army.)

it was fitting to have Ronnie McDevitt make the presentation. 'Bonnie Ronnie' had missed only two Scotland away games in Europe, against East Germany and Malta, since 1977. The Faroes was Ronnie's seventy-first Scotland game on foreign soil. Counting pre-World Cup friendlies, the opening game against Brazil in France '98 will be Ronnie's eighty-eighth away game.

'I remember Mr McLaren a few years ago at an under 21s game in Bulle,' declared Rab Irvine as the presentation got underway, 'he was not a happy man then.'

The game had taken place near Berne, Switzerland, and Rab had treated spectators to some fine footballing skills during the half time break. Big Rab, a taxi driver in London, is, to say the least, a big man. Not unlike the *Tango* man in the old TV orange

The Wizard: dives with the speed of a coiled hippo.

drink advert. Rab, or 'The Grand Wizard' as he is often known, dresses differently from his Tango cousin and comes fully equipped in tartan suit, topped off with a tartan tea cosy with a small Saltire and Lion Rampant protruding from each side of this headgear. The Wizard has established himself as a serial appearer in the national and international press, and has the framed pictures to prove it hanging up and down the length of his home in Charlton in London.

At half time in Bulle, The Wizard decided to demonstrate his goalkeeping skills. He promptly took to the pitch and established himself between the posts. Five Scotland reserves began firing in shots which the big man, showing all the dexterity and speed of a coiled hippo, dived left and right to tip the balls past the posts. No doubt in their frustration that our national football representatives were unable to subdue the Wizard, other Tartan Army took the field to show them how it should be done.

They were all joined by an extremely irate Mr McLaren who, as Head Security Advisor at the SFA, was there to ensure that none of the fans seriously tarnished the good name of Scotland.

'What are you up to you big eejit?' demanded Mr McLaren, despite the obvious. The Wizard was indignant.

'And who the hell do you think your talking to? Who are you callin' an eejit? Don't forget, I pay your wages.'

Later while the Wizard was drinking beers at a small wooden hut at the side of the park he saw three men in long coats approaching. 'Aw naw, here comes more hassle.' Wrong. Mr McLaren, accompanied by a couple of officials was not on the warpath.

'Listen, I was a bit out of order. It was just when the others came on. In fact we were thoroughly enjoying your goalkeeping.' The Wizard's goodwill message on the card Bonnie Ronnie handed to Mr McLaren read 'from your goalkeeper in Bulle.'

The Grand Wizard had to use more than a little guile to get himself onto the Wembley turf in '77. By the time he pushed his way down to the front he didnae have enough energy left to scramble over the tiny wall that separated him from the turf which had, over the previous ninety minutes, rocketed in value. Also, he was a considerable distance from either of the goals which were really occupying his attention. If in doubt, summon help. So the big fella appeared to pass out, attracting the attention of medics who struggled and heaved to haul the limp body over the wall and onto a stretcher.

Well I guess some of Rab must have been on the stretcher as the unfortunate stretcher bearers slowly negotiated the seemingly unconscious Wizard along the track. When they eventually got as close as they were going to be to one of the goals Rab sprang up with a shout, 'Stop!' He declared that he felt much better now and waddled off onto the densely populated turf. Rab insists that somehow he managed to get up onto the goals, conceding that it took the help of many hands, and that it was his bulk which finally broke the crossbar.

The game against Scotland was a big event in the Faroes. Close to 10 per cent of the national population was there in a crowd of around 4,000. Scotland were two up by half time and the Tartan Dolphins danced above the heads of the small contingent of Scottish fans. During the second 45 minutes the hosts put us under some pressure and created a few worrying moments. But there was no further scoring or the need for the kind of drastic measures Big Tattie, otherwise known as 'Kinlochbervie', had resorted to over a decade earlier on another island some miles to

Dolphin goes mad when Scotland score.

the north. The occasion was an under 21 game in Iceland and a glance up at the wooden scoreboard told that the Scots were behind. Kinlochbervie felt an irresistible call to action. Climbing the scoreboard ladder he lifted a number 3 from the pile of

Game? What game?

numbers, withdrew the offending digit '0' and slotted in a hat trick for Scotland. Having had enough of the game, Kinlochbervie then slipped quietly from the ground. About a minute later he heard a cheer coming from the remaining Scotland fans. It was not the equaliser, they had just noticed the scoreboard.

It felt like Iceland at the Faroes game. Even light winds made the exposed stadium bitterly cold. Seemingly oblivious to this was Findlay from Muir of Ord who was standing with his pal wee Chizzy. Both are short and very stocky guys with the kind of necks that would make them very difficult to hang. Findlay in particular didn't mind the climatic conditions and wore only a waistcoat on top, a picture which appeared on the front of the daily newspaper the following morning. Craig (Shaky) Steven from Edinburgh was probably well pleased that he was wearing his Mig fighter pilot's helmet acquired in Moscow.

The Muir of Ord Boys:
many are cauld, but few are frozen.

There was a nice moment in the second half when Craig was standing just beyond the corner flag chatting to two seven year old Faroese kids. Scotland won a corner, one of few successes in the second half, and John Collins ran over to take the kick. As he was reaching for the ball he glanced up at the threesome deep in conversation. He could hardly take the kick for laughing. Craig was showing the kids how the electronic visor went up and down. The weans were nodding enthusiastically, mock red hair spilling out from under their 'See you Jimmy' hats. At this point Johnny Marr stepped forward from the crowd and fired a kid's bow and arrow at the Scotland midfielder. Now John Collins is a fine striker of the dead ball, but this effort did not turn out to be one of his best.

As the fans descended the hill after the game the sight below was like a mini Dunkirk. A flotilla of small boats fanned its way out to sea as the Faroese made for their homes on the surrounding islands. The light was magical. It looked like there was a hole in the sky as a large beam of light streamed down onto the ocean.

We are sailing, we are sailing: the Tartan Navy ready to disembark.

'Ah, so that's where they hid the Holy Grail. Thought no-one would find it up here,' muttered one Scot who obviously had been indulging heavily in Gull Export Beer.

One of the boats might have been the *Amadeus*. We forgot to ask when we hired it the following afternoon. I think the *Amadeus* was Stef's idea. Secure in the company of several crates of the trusty Gull, about fifteen of us boarded the craft and set out to sea. The captain sailed us close to the highest and most stunning cliffs I've ever seen, but the troops were demanding whale.

'We want to see a minke whale,' yelled Schillachi, the spray soaking the lenses of his round John Lennon-type specks and the old pair of sandshoes he always wears with the kilt.

'We're all minky here,' grunted Mad Dog.

The search for whale proved fruitless and after about four hours the boat returned to port. The sea can grow on you. Bonnie Ronnie, videoing the final few hundred yards of the *Amadeus's* return, could make out Mad Harry from Peterhead swinging from the top of the mast and was shocked to hear the following verse wafting across the waves:

Ye cin stick yir Tartan Army up yir arse,
Ye cin stick yir Tartan Army up yir arse,
Ye cin stick yir Tartan Army,
Cause we're the TARTAN NAVY,
Ye cin stick yir Tartan Army up yir arse.

But everything was soon back to normal when Mad Dog announced, 'Shore leave for all hands'.

It got pretty cold out there on the open sea and life jackets were donned for heat. The captain didn't appear to mind as Four Fingers, looking like a beach ball on legs, kept his on when we left the boat. Come to think of it the Faroese didn't seem to mind about anything you did. The next time I saw Four Fingers I was surprised to find him without the life jacket. But that was a few months later in Copenhagen. The jacket was glued to him for the duration of his time in the Faroes and I hear he raised eyebrows two days later squeezing along the aisle of the plane on the flight home.

The Faroes offer marvellous opportunities for walkers and the rugged beauty of the landscape is a magnet to painters, artists and photographers. There were none of these talents among Tam Scones, Joker, Bruce and Wee Geordie, but the foursome still set off from the Youth Hostel relishing the prospect of a healthy hike in the hills. After a while their progress was impeded by a large fence. Undaunted, they skirted along it for a while until they found a gap that looked big enough to squeeze under. It was not a good idea for big Bruce to go first, or indeed go at all. The other three might have made it but Bruce had no chance. Stuck and wriggling it was at that point they discovered that it was an electric fence. Bruce got little sympathy from his fellow hikers. Wee Geordie was even caught with a lustful look in his eye. These were obviously desperate men.

Bruce was free by the Friday afternoon as the *Smyril* prepared for the return sail to Aberdeen. A few of our new friends were at the quayside to wave the troops goodbye. One of our new friends, Suzy from Amsterdam to be precise, was sailing with us. Suzy had shown a great affection for the Tartan Army and had being doing everything humanly and physically possible to obtain honourary membership. I'm pretty sure she managed it.

I think it was Dougie (The Orc) Graham and Davie (Kunta Kintae) McLymons who met Suzy first. These two would put any normal lady off, so it just shows how keen she was to gain her stripes. Suzy and her mother had come to the Faroes to see the cliffs and pass a quiet couple of weeks. After encountering the Orc and Kunta Kintae (a psychiatric nurse) her mother never saw Suzy for the rest of the vacation. The poor woman, her movement slightly handicapped by a clubbed foot, was regularly spotted hobbling around Torshaven searching for her daughter for the best part of the week.

'Have you seen my daughter Suzy? I think she is with some of your friends.' It was a damned shame. The daughter was a volunteer with no chance of a dishonourable discharge. The next time they would see each other would be on the *Smyril* on the way back to Aberdeen.

Suzy was certainly something special. Back on board the *Smyril*, I asked her about her career plans as we waited at the island of Suderoy for a coffin to be taken off. This was an unscheduled stop. Earlier in the day, on the way to Torshaven, someone had fallen, or thrown themselves, overboard and drowned. It had been a sombre sail from Torshaven to Suderoy and there was a tangible nervousness among the fans. The bar, which had been open for the full duration of the outward sail, remained closed.

The Orc added to the growing sense of unease by speculating that 'maybe the guy had the bar keys in his pocket when he went overboard.'

Luckily it was a false alarm. Once we got shot of the coffin the party started again. The band played long and loud and the only further threat to the festivities was when the Orc attempted to relieve the female vocalist of the mike, lost his balance and went crashing, with the singer in tow, headfirst into the group's equipment.

However, the brief respite gave a few of us a chance to ask Suzy about herself. She was 21 years old and on a Business Studies course.

'What do you see yourself doing when you finish,' I asked her.

'I want to open up a delicatessen shop in Amsterdam,' Suzy replied.

'Oh yeah? I bet I know what kind of shop that will be,' Tam Scones chipped in. 'Groceries in the front shop and sausages through the back.'

She threw us a disapproving look (which was rich). 'I know what you mean,' she said, but offered no further details about her business aspirations. Suzy might be walking like John Wayne, but she had her head screwed on too.

We were now 12 hours into the return voyage and I was catching a breath of fresh air in the company of Alan Jamieson and Stevie Clark from the Shetland island of Yell. We were staring out into the mist.

'Keen dis, Andy,' says Alan, 'Yell is ower yunder. Just a peerie minute away.' Alan and the rest of the Shetland boys had another 12 hours to go to Aberdeen, a flight back to Shetland and then another boat to Yell in front of them. Even going to a Scotland home game is like a foreign campaign for these lads.

'Not to worry Alan, it's been a memorable trip and the *Smyril* folk have been great to us. You know, going by ferry has not always been so smooth,' I said, smiling as I recalled one of Tommy Madden's previous experiences. This had been back in October 1986 when a blanket ban on football fans by ferry companies threatened the plans of the Partick Thistle International Supporters Section who were relying on seaborne transportation to get them to a game against Eire in Dublin. Undeterred, they got themselves together and formed *The Summerston Young Farmers Association*.

Summerston is in the Maryhill part of Glasgow, not a place famous for farming activity. Therefore, if questioned by the ferry operator about the purpose of their journey, the 'Association' had

Big Bruce gets the Horn in the Faroes.

taken steps to demonstrate that they were, in fact, on their way to visit agricultural co-operatives in Ireland with a view to establishing an inner city farm in Maryhill. Just to be sure that their appearance was in fitting with this mission, the Association members all turned up at the ferry terminal for the Cairnryan - Larne crossing wearing welly boots, carrying copies of *Farmers Weekly*, and sporting official looking badges marked *Summerston Young Farmers, FARMEX '86, Dublin*. Several other coach loads of fans were turned away, but the Tartan farmers made the crossing which passed without incident.

As they were disembarking, one of the crew remarked 'Enjoy the game lads'.

CHAPTER 4

THE CAMPER VAN FROM HELL

AFTER THE MANY HAPPY MEMORIES OF EURO '92, the Tartan Army were looking forward to returning return to Sweden for the friendly in Stockholm in October '95 with great anticipation. The turnout at the game (a 2:0 defeat) was around 400, much smaller than the great support that had followed Scotland in Sweden back in '92. The three away games between March and June in Moscow, San Marino and the Faroe Islands had punched a serious hole in people's pockets. Many bits of plastic had been recalled by their banking owners. For some of the Scots lads, this game was effectively a home one. Like big Eddie O'Gorman who had married a Swedish girl and was living on the edge of the Arctic Circle with their baby boy. And we soon found out that Eddie was not the only one who was building a new life in this foreign country in the aftermath of Scotland's campaign of '92.

For a group of us including myself, Auld Davie, Johnny Marr, Graeme (Psycho Sid) Aitken, Tam (Four Fingers) Ritchie, Chiz Bear, and Davie Lewis, the Swedish friendly had, on the face of it, some signs of being a relatively quiet and organised affair. A camper van had been booked for a week. It was scheduled for collection in Malmo in southern Sweden on the Saturday after we had sampled the delights of Copenhagen. We were faced with a lengthy and sober drive north to Stockholm. As the SFA's 'Guidance Notes' to travelling fans pointed out 'the consumption of alcoholic drinks in public places is not allowed by law,' and 'Sweden's laws on drinking and driving are strictly enforced...

you will be prosecuted if you have only consumed the equivalent of half a can of normal beer.' Also, as Doug Graham, the infamous Orc who had plagued the Faroe Islands, had decided against making the trip late in the day, our little band was minus a serious miscreant. But we should have known better. I mean, for a start, Johnny Marr was there!

The trip started OK. Auld Davie and me made our scheduled tea time plane on Friday afternoon from Glasgow to Copenhagen, a more successful start than Ian Graham and his pals Paul, Kenny and Ian from Denny who we met at Glasgow Airport and remembered from Moscow. They were on their way for a week of Swedish hospitality in a small village by the name of Krylbo, near the town of Avesta. Some Swedish friends they had first met during Italia '90 were waiting to collect them at Stockholm airport. The Swedes had been waiting all day as the Scots should have caught an early morning flight. At least the Denny boys proved to be consistent. They also missed their plane home a week later.

For us the trip started to go wrong as soon as we arrived at Copenhagen Airport. Chiz was waiting to greet us as we came through customs. The last time I'd seen Chiz had been at Glenfinnan in August for the 250th anniversary of Bonnie Prince Charlie's landing on mainland Scotland and the raising of the Jacobite standard. The Highland Games that day had attracted a fair turnout from the Tartan Army. Meeting Chiz at the airport unexpectedly was great. But getting robbed of £800 in foreign currency by a pickpocket as we swallowed a few beers at the airport bar sucked. It ruined our

Chiz is gutted to hear about my £800 getting stolen... he'd been hoping for a sub.

night. Well, for about ten minutes it did. By the time we arrived in the Shamrock Bar in the centre of Copenhagen to meet the rest of the lads, who had a full day's headstart on us, it was about 10pm and the troops were in full swing.

Johnny Marr had already had a slight mishap earlier that morning. Having retired prematurely to his hotel room in pieces, he rose in the wee hours in need of the toilet and set off down the corridor with only his duvet to hide his modesty. When the rest of the lads woke a few hours later there was no sign of Johnny. Surely after the state he had been in he couldn't be up, washed and away so early in the morning?

The boys soon found out that Johnny was still in the hotel. In fact he was on the same corridor, only a few doors away. They heard a furious commotion. Psycho Sid, a fellow member of the Edinburgh Tartan Army, opened the door to see what was going on and there was Johnny in full flight, duvet flapping. He was being chased by an irate guy attempting to unload what looked to be a rally of kung fu blows. Johnny had lost his way coming back from the toilet a few hours earlier and ended up bedding down in the wrong room where a guy and two women were already asleep. This was the guy just waking up and trying to inform Johnny of his mistake.

Copenhagen is a city which never sleeps. Four Fingers and me drifted away from the pack to sample several hostelries, starting off in the company of two local ladies who presented themselves as enthusiastic tour guides. After a short drive we ended up in a dark cavernous joint with multiple bars and disco areas. Four Fingers spotted me deep in conversation with a long leggy customer with a skirt that resembled a scarf and showing a generous amount of suspender. Four Fingers was soon hauling at my arm.

'Come on Andy, we'd better go.'

'Piss off Tam. We're no long here an ah'm gettin' on just fine.'

'No, no Andy, you don't understand, that's a guy you're talking to. Let's get the hell out of here now.' Tam was bang on. Our helpful tour guides had brought us to one of the biggest gay clubs in Copenhagen. We knew it was big because we got lost trying to get out. And we knew it was gay because of the attention our kilts were attracting from characters who certainly could not be confused with the fairer sex. We made sure we were more selective in our choice of establishments for the rest of the morning.

In the course of grabbing some breakfast in Burger King, Four Fingers ended up in conversation with Peter Schmichael, Manchester United's Danish international goalkeeper. He was with his minders who were reluctant to let this strange sight near their prized asset. Four Fingers persisted.

'I'm only going to have a few words with Peter, I know him.' In his capacity as a taxi driver back in Stockport, Four Fingers was right. The Schmichael family used his taxi firm on a regular basis. Well poor Peter was soon very spooked as Tam proceeded to tell him where he lived, his wife's name and what she looked like, private stuff right down to the street number and name of his house. Maybe Peter should have been impressed, but after a short reflection Tam reckoned he wasn't and concluded that he had just lost his taxi firm a valued client.

Meanwhile big Davie Lewis, who refers to himself as anorexic, was sitting outside some other bizarre establishment throwing up. This was not due to his medical condition. I should stress that

Davie believes he is anorexic, not bulimic. It was because he had accepted some substance from an Irish lady which was not of dark, liquid form. He realises now he should have stuck with the Guinness.

When people meet big Davie, who weighs around 17 stone, it comes as rather a shock to hear him declare he is anorexic.

'Why do you think you're anorexic?' folk usually ask.

Big Davie: eating for Scotland.

'Well,' explains Davie, 'when an anorexic looks in the mirror they think they're fat. When I look in a mirror so do I. So I must be anorexic.' Fair enough. Davie was certainly not on a healthy eating tour. He found it virtually impossible to pass a kebab shop throughout the whole campaign.

By the time Four Fingers and me made it back to the Hotel Centrum, one of many hotels near the railway station in a district peppered with sex shops and pokey drinking establishments with names like the Spunk Bar, the rest of the boys had left for the ferry to Malmo in southern Sweden. When some of us returned to Copenhagen over a week later we had time to visit the Spunk Bar, but found it a great disappointment. It was unable to meet our request for four pints of its home brew. But just now Tam and I had no time to hang around. It was close to mid-day Saturday and we had a camper van to collect in Malmo and five missing troops to find. Being unable to convince a charming blonde lady with tattoos and rings through several parts of her anatomy to act as the van's mascot and accompany us to the game, and after having purchased her a ticket for the ferry, we made the sea crossing to Malmo alone. Marr, Auld Davie, Big Davie, Psycho Sid and Chiz were found outside a pub in Malmo, as usual by accident rather than design.

The camper van trip did not start well. Things started to fall apart inside the vehicle fairly quickly. Tables collapsed, cupboards were broken, curtains were ripped, lights were smashed and, after Johnny Marr and Four Fingers had insisted that no one should shit in the toilet, Johnny Marr and Four Fingers took turns to shit in the toilet. The pollution did not help the atmosphere in the camper van. By the time the party reached Norkopping late in the evening, four of us checked into the Hotel Princess for the night. We were of a mind to pull the plug on the whole campaign, forget the van and fly home direct the following day.

Disposal of the vehicle occupied the conversation that evening and the following morning. Mr. Rassmussan, the camper van owner, had all our details and passport numbers, so simply abandoning the vehicle wasn't really on. Then Psycho Sid came up with the more attractive idea of driving it to Oslo where England were due to play a friendly and setting it alight. It would be insured, so the owner wouldn't lose out. At least we'd get to see a bit of Norway and the English fans would get the blame for gratuitous vandalism. But then again, they would probably appreciate the gesture.

The discussion continued as the van set off for Stockholm to dispose of the three who aimed to stay for the game. It was a quieter group now. Chiz and Johnny had spent hours walking around Norkopping in the dead of night looking for the camper van which had been left in a car park in the centre of the town. They had left Four Fingers sleeping in a corner in the Palace Disco, yet he got back to the van hours before them. The pair eventually stumbled on the police station, announced they were lost, and proceeded to be as helpful as they could possibly be.

'What does the van look like?' asked the policeman taking details.

'It's white,' replied Johnny.

'I think it's a Toyota,' added Chiz, not even remotely close.

'And can you describe the place you left it?'

'It's surrounded by buildings,' announced Chiz with a little more accuracy. The lost pair then monopolised one of only three police cars on duty that night. Some time later Four Fingers awoke to two policemen banging on the camper van door at six in the morning.

'Do you have two friends who look like you?' This, of course, is quite impossible. Four Fingers having friends and lookalikes! Kilts are the only common feature.

Time is a great healer. By the time the camper van party reached Stockholm around mid afternoon on the Sunday, attitudes had softened and plans for a retreat were quietly dropped. The journey had not been altogether unpleasant. The scenery was good and Andy Stewart was belting out all his old favourites. Even Johnny was beginning to make some sense talking about his hopes for the European Championships the coming June. In his sleep he could see Scotland lifting the Cup after a glorious victory over the host nation at Wembley.

'Don't you ever get them Andy,' he asked, 'you know, dreams that sometimes come true.'

'No Johnny, I'm afraid not. It's usually the nightmares that come true for me.'

The camper van did not serve its intended purpose as a source of cheap, mobile accommodation. Rooms were secured in the Hotel Danielson in Stockholm and the camper van was abandoned in a nearby side street. This van saw quite a few side streets during its time in Sweden with its contingent of the Tartan Army. In addition to performing a valuable role as an inter-city taxi service, it helped keep a fleet of Swedish traffic wardens gainfully employed as it collected parking tickets all around the country.

Come to think of it, hotel rooms didn't serve as sleeping quarters either. When sleep was had, which was not often, it tended to be the odd hour or two in the corner of some pub or nightclub. Now and again you managed a quick kip in someone else's room or in a park, because the weather was unexpectedly clement. But hotels came in handy as we needed somewhere secure to dump our bags. For the Tartan Army, Swedish hotel rooms represent some of the most expensive left luggage facilities in Europe.

On occasions the van did come in useful as a location for early morning parties. However, at the start of the week the parties tended to be short lived: a legacy of Four Fingers' and Johnny Marr's indiscretion. Something had to be done about the toilet, and it fell to Big Davie, Psycho Sid and myself. We deserved medals for slopping out the now putrid bog. This exercise took place down at the docks. The stench was sickening, which explains why Big Davie was sick. After a few days the stuff that Tam and Johnny had left behind had taken on a life of its own and was very reluctant to leave. As it was eventually discharged into the Baltic Sea, worry spread among our responsible section of the Tartan Army that we might be to blame for starting a cholera outbreak in Stockholm.

A lot of the revelry in Stockholm took place in the Dubliner pub to the rear of the Grand Hotel, a cheap place which charged a mere £5 for a watery pint of Guinness. Maybe that explains why it was common to see Tartan Army turning their pints into more interesting concoctions. One particularly elaborate and nourishing effort contained a full leak, lettuce and other assorted vegetables, and a generous handful of prawns. Big Davie was spotted consuming most of this one. Kebabs were in short supply in the Dubliner. The bands were good but the floor show was often better. Robert Dickie from Glasgow played the pipes as he

Rocking the Dubliner Bar in Stockholm.

swapped his kilt for a Swedish girl's skirt and didn't miss a note. On quieter moments, Johnny Marr introduced party games, like bar diving. Johnny had great faith in two of his mates who acted as catchers, but faith failed to break Johnny's fall. Time and time again he dived from the end of the bar and crashed through the four outstretched arms. When he got home, people thought he had a tan, albeit an uneven one. Wrong. You don't get a tan from bar diving, only lumps and bruises.

Better still than the Dubliner floor show was to see, once again, so many seasoned footsoldiers. Many of the faces don't have real names: nicknames, but not christian ones and surnames. Now and again you wonder how someone has acquired their nickname, but in other cases not much is left to the imagination. A case in point would be Kenny Nicol of the London Scottish. Kenny is widely known as 'Captain Vodka.'

You do see many of the troops at home matches, especially if you book your tickets early enough and give Marjory Nimmo enough time to locate you with the rest of the travelling support. But then again not all of Scotland's travelling support attend home games. Some of the regular travellers live in remote locations, like Estonia, Belgium, Costa Rica and Canada and are more likely to be spotted enjoying the carnival atmosphere at away games. A few others stay away from certain grounds on a point of principle, like Paddy from Dunfermline who was once denied entry to a game at Hampden by the Glasgow Polis on account of the snare drum he was carrying. Paddy protested on grounds of liberty and freedom. Furthermore, the drum had been in Mexico and had played in the slums of Netza. It had also led 'The March' of thousands to the Sweden game in Genoa in 1990. The Glasgow Polis were unimpressed and denied Paddy his liberty for the evening.

Shetlanders: never seen a camera before.

There were also new faces to meet in the Dubliner. The Shetland boys from Yell numbered seven on this occasion: the four regulars (Alan Jamieson, Stevie Clark, Colin Clark and Owen Strachan) and three new recruits. They had travelled to Stockholm via Helsinki to rekindle fond memories of the trip to Finland just over a year before. New blood is essential for the survival of the Tartan Army. There are always casualties along the way. Folk do not come home, some by choice, others because they get stranded and can't get back. After a major campaign like the finals of the World Cup or European Championships, Marjory Nimmo can expect to receive several inquiries from irate wives, calling the SFA and wanting to know what has become of their husbands who should have been home days or weeks before.

One case involved a guy from Clydebank who had been in Sweden for the '92 Euro Finals. On arriving home he informed his wife that he no longer loved her and was leaving. He had met the woman of his dreams and was returning to Sweden to spend the rest of his life with her. He packed his case, packed in his job and off he went. It was not long after this that Andy Roxburgh's letter to the Tartan Army arrived in the post. On reading Andy's congratulations for our excellent behaviour during the Finals, and hearing that her estranged husband was in fact an 'ambassador for his country,' the lady's patience finally snapped. She hit the roof and promptly got on the phone to the SFA.

'What does the manager of the national team think he's playing at sending me a letter telling me how good my husband is? Ambassador? Let me tell you what he is. He's no any Ambassador.

He's a total bastard. He's just left me and the weans for some Swedish bimbo.' Once again it was poor Marjory who had to field the call. The postscript is that it didn't quite work out for this tartan romeo. Some months later he reappeared in Clydebank subdued and repentant, and with a massive repair job on his hands.

There are domestic casualties too, as people get themselves married, have kids, and show that there are still Scots fans capable of showing responsibility to the family unit. However, for many troops a withdrawal from active service is only a temporary phenomenon. Responsibility has its limits. Families grow up. People forget how sick they felt watching Scotland get beat. For whatever reason, faces reappear years later to take up their position once again on the terracing.

But footsoldiers can and do go missing in action for a variety of other reasons quite apart from romance. A most bizarre tale was sent to me by a Mr Sid Green, a member of the London Scottish. I have been reassured by others from the London Scottish of the authenticity of this strange account, but it still seems scarcely believable. Here it is in Mr Green's own words:

> Ken and Jill Hine are an English married couple, both in their late 30s and qualified English teachers. For the past 20 years they have led a nomadic life, travelling extensively and working as teachers in their host countries. During 1990, while travelling overland through South America en route to taking up teaching jobs in Peru and finding that they were well ahead of schedule, they decided to break their journey in Ecuador for a couple of weeks and explore the country's interior.
>
> From the capital, Quito, they ventured eastwards towards the Napo region, where they knew the terrain would be thick with jungle. The only way in was by small boat, capable of navigating the winding rivers and tributaries which dissect the land. Few people have reason or opportunity to make this slow, arduous and potentially hazardous journey. They were fortunate and met a boat owner who was travelling deep into the region to trade with the natives. For a small fee, he agreed to take them along.
>
> They journeyed for several days, occasionally stopping at small, riverside communities, usually consisting of a few ramshackle wooden huts with no power or sanitation. Well into the trip, at

one such outpost, they stopped for an hour or two. There was a large hut where the provisions were stored which served as the main meeting place. Upon entering they were warmly greeted by a group of natives, the type of which they had become accustomed. They wore brightly coloured wrap around blankets and either Bowler or Welsh chimney style hats. Several had grotesquely distorted lips, the result of having half moon shaped wooden slats inserted into them.

Ken and Jill were surprised to spot a tall bearded man in his early 40s obviously of European descent. He wore a kilt and a tee-shirt, both well past their best, and on the shirt they could just make out, in faded print, 'Ally's Army'. He could speak the native language and he was equally surprised to meet them. He explained that he was from Scotland and had been there since 1978, the result of exploring, getting lost and losing his valuables while making his way overland from the USA to Argentina for the World Cup Finals. He had flown to the States and then travelled overland through Mexico and Central America, Guatemala, El Salvador, Honduras, Nicaragua, Costa Rica, Panama and Colombia. His epic journey had halted approximately 3,500 miles from the U.S.A, 2,500 miles from the border with Argentina and 4,100 miles from Buenos Aires.

They were the first English speaking people he had met in 12 years. During this time he had not read a newspaper, listened to a radio or had any substantive form of communication with the wider world. Ken and Jill normally lived away from Britain and had no interest in football. So they could not enlighten him as to how the Scotland team had been doing. They did not even know who had won the cup in 1978 or how far Scotland had progressed.

They offered him assistance in leaving, at least as far as Quito, but he declined insisting he was okay where he was. After a few drinks Ken and Jill returned to the boat, Quito and on to Peru. Ken recently recounted this event to his brother who lives in England. Ken and Jill are now teaching in North Korea. Unfortunately neither of them can recall the Scotsman's name, or where in Scotland he came from.

Ian Munro, a highlander from Strathy in northernmost Sutherland, failed to return from Italy in 1990. The reason? He found gainful employment.

'I got myself a job in a bank in Turin,' Ian recalls proudly. Anyone who knows Munro will appreciate the surprise with which this information is normally met. Munro, though a gentle soul, has a fierce appearance and a face like a horse hair sporran. Not your archetypal bank teller. But the story gains plausibility as Munro continues and explains that he was the bank's window cleaner. This member of the Tartan Army was standing in for a year while the regular employee was off doing national service in the Italian Army.

Munro is a seasoned campaigner and really merits a chapter on his own. Over several beers in Athens in December 1994, I asked Ian if it was true that he'd sold his house in Glasgow to get to Mexico in 1986 without his

Ian Munro, Highlander: Anyone want to buy a house? (Don't tell the wife.)

wife knowing, that is until the lawyers for the new owners came looking for the keys. Broadly speaking it was. Anne Diamond and Nick Owen, the presenters of Breakfast TV, had also got wind of the story from Glasgow lass Loraine Kelly and Ian was invited to guest on the show. Viewers of the encounter recall two very nervous interviewers and an increasingly frustrated Scotsman who, hit with a series of lame questions, was not being given the chance to get his message over.

Questions like 'So you are going to Mexico to support Scotland?' and 'We understand you sold your house to pay for the trip. Is that not a bit extreme?' were not helping Ian get started. 'Look,' said Munro, 'you may not get to the World Cup again, but you can always get yourself another house.' He then expanded.

'I enjoy travelling overland to the games. I like to take the time to see other countries. I like meeting the local people and getting to understand their ways. And I like a good drink.' Munro was doing his best to outline his philosophy on life as expressed through the Tartan Army, but it fell on deaf ears as Anne, believing Munro to be thirsty, reached for a jug and poured him an orange juice.

During a later meeting with Munro, when I'd been talking about our jaunt around Sweden in the Camper Van from Hell, he reciprocated with recollections of the famous Park Bar Bus which had transported him to the '82 World Cup in Spain. The bus was a 1961 Bedford, bought by Johnny Morrison from Inverness for the princely sum of £400 when it was a virtual wreck and a home to nesting birds. Originally a 29 seater, it was modified to carry 13 Tartan Army. A cooker was installed, a beer font placed over the sink and seat number 27 was converted into a toilet with tartan curtains. The Park Bar Bus became a legend as it rattled its way to Scotland away games throughout the 1980s. The vehicle had a habit of shedding important components. Dozing during one night drive, Munro suspected the shearing noise was announcing the loss of a pretty essential part and alerted the rest of the bus with a variation of a song popularised by American folk singer, Kenny Rogers, 'You picked a fine time to leave me loose wheel. It's 4 in the morning...'

The Park Bar Bus kept itself occupied in between Scotland games. For a time it hosted a team of construction workers who were building a bridge in the Highlands. However, not everyone was happy with the arrangement. Preparing for a Royal visit to the area, the local council formed the opinion that the bus detracted from the amenity value of the area and insisted that this 'eyesore' be removed from the side of the road. But the grand old vehicle ended its service with the Tartan Army with style. It carried a 'Plaque of Friendship' from the Lord Provost of Inverness to his counterpart in Genoa during Italia '90. After that she was retired and sold for £1,500 to a group of German students: nearly four times what Johnny Morrison had paid for her almost a decade earlier.

But let me get back to Stockholm and the main focus of this chapter. It was in the Dubliner on the Monday afternoon that someone came up with the idea of taking in a movie. *Braveheart* was showing at the Rigaletto cinema at 7pm. Just the very dab to get us out of the pub for a wee while. So come 6.30pm around sixty of the Tartan Army in full regalia made their way towards the Rigaletto, picking up some stray Swedes on the way. The locals must have thought that this was the cast of *Braveheart* in Stockholm for the premiere. The cinema was packed. Even the aisles were full.

This was audience involvement par excellence. Every time one of the opposition got whacked by Wallace, total pandemonium. Edward Longshank's son, him who became Edward the Second and was comprehensively gubbed by the Bruce at Bannockburn, first appeared on screen at his wedding to a beautiful French princess. But it was clear young Eddie's affections lay elsewhere as he made intimate eye contact with a young gent at his rear. Of course this audience spotted Eddie right away.

'There's Jimmy Hill!' which started the cinema on a rendition of the legendary song. Out of the darkness, one voice was heard to shout, 'Yes Jimmy, you can run, you can even kit yourself out in medieval dress, but you cannot hide from the Tartan Army.'

At one point in the screening, just towards the end of the Battle of Stirling Bridge, the movie stopped, the lights went on and concerned management staff appeared. They must have suspected a full scale war was going on. The noise was so great that it had disturbed some of the other viewers. But these were viewers watching films being shown in other cinemas in the complex. All in all it was a great way to see a no bad film of Scotland's great patriot and there was hardly a dry eye in the house.

The spirit of Wallace has proved a source of fortitude to Tartan Army footsoldiers and in many situations. Gus Clark was deemed unfit for active service in Sweden at the last minute. The trouble was noticed towards the end of Gus's shift on a building site in Edinburgh. A mildly uncomfortable sensation just inside his bum quickly developed into an affliction so painfully debilitating that by the time he shuffled into the Royal Infirmary he needed a wheelchair.

'I must have a boil in ma bum,' Gus informed the nurse. A doctor conducted a closer and more knowingful inspection.

'No, Mr Clark, you have an anal abscess which requires immediate emergency surgery.' Gus, who had been planning to take his lovely wife June out that evening to see *Braveheart* for the fifth time, found himself whisked off to the Eastern General Hospital, stripped and draped in a white gown and prepared for the knife.

On coming to his senses the following morning, Gus was met with smiles all round, from patients and nurses alike.

'You were on good form last night.' 'Much better than the telly.' Gus had no idea what they were on about. It turned out that he had put on a bit of a show while still half whacked out by the anaesthetic. Throughout the night he had been springing up in bed with loud proclamations.

'Don't you worry son. You be proud to be a Jambo.' The subconscious trigger had been a young Hearts fan in the next bed. Gus had been speaking to him just before being wheeled off to theatre.

'I want a half bottle of vodka and a poke a chips.' Gus had come straight from work and hadn't eaten for hours. Scotland and *Braveheart* were also at work in his mental processes. 'We'll be there in June.' 'The McDonalds, the McLeods, the Camerons are goin' over the top.' 'You can take our lives, but you can never take our Freedom.' Gus's operation was a complete success, but while the Tartan Army was giving it laldy in the Rigaletto Cinema the convalescent was back in Edinburgh eating his tea off the mantlepiece.

Getting to the game against Sweden was organised chaos. Most of the troops correctly chose the underground as the quickest and most efficient mode of transport. Well it should have been. The Rasunda stadium was just a few stops away and required no change of train. It took most of the fans two or three changes. A few were extremely lucky to get there at all. There was very nearly a nasty incident on a descending escalator. A group of footsoldiers, including the overjoyed Eddie O'Gorman, who had been sitting and chatting during the descent failed in their bid to stand up to get off and approached the escalator's teeth in a heap. Onlookers had visions of kilts and scrotums being devoured by the machine. It was thanks to the quick reaction of a couple of fans, who were only very drunk, that disaster was averted.

Given such dangers during the outward journey, it is not

surprising that a couple of fans, with a Swede in tow, sought alternative transportation for the return leg. This came in the form of a white stretch limousine with smoked glass windows and equipped with TV and crystal glasses. The vehicle was on hire outside of the stadium. Who knows who the driver was expecting, but he had no qualms about his passengers so long as

they had Visa. As the limo made its way slowly through the crowd, Russell Ritchie was spotted stoatin' along on his own.

'Pull over please, and give this man a lift.' Russell saw the car slowing down and thought, 'Hey, Rod must be in town. Nice

Call me a cab? OK, you're a cab.

of him to stop.' The smoked glass window went down slowly and a ba heid, topped with a green Balmoral bunnet and feathers, popped out.

There were other bizarre sights to be seen around town that night. One fan was spotted outside of the Dubliner talking to a half wolf and its Texan owner. The same eejit was later seen with the same wolf and Texan in a fancy coffee shop. By this time the beast was wearing a tartan scarf and was being spoon fed a large slice of blueberry pie by its new found friend. Marr and Kenny (The General) Reid purchased their own pets: invisible animals, each wearing a collar fixed at the end of a long stiff metal leash. But give them their due. They took good care of their pets and were seen leaving Sloppies night club at regular intervals to let the non-existent dogs relieve themselves.

Outside Sloppies, another Scot met a down and out Swedish female. All this poor girl had was a poncho and a few bits and pieces: a lipstick, a hair brush, some other toiletries and a shirt. This was her home. All her worldly possessions. The Scot fancied a night out in the fresh air himself and was trying to buy the lot.

The lady was refusing to sell, so he emptied his sporran of its contents and wished her the best of fortune. Meanwhile a handful of fans left the nightclub with a more affluent lady who was taking them home for a group sauna. Following Scotland is a dirty, sweaty business and fans need to take every opportunity that presents itself to get themselves cleaned up.

The camper van left Stockholm on Thursday, the day after the match, bound for Gothenburg. The group was minus Chiz, who had declared himself unfit to travel and remained behind in the Dubliner in the company of

Barking fans with invisible dogs in Sloppies.

Eddie O'Gorman. Certainly, not a strategy for recovery. Chiz reappeared at Copenhagen airport the following Sunday, a shivering, shaking wreck. He was not due to travel till the Monday but had bought another flight so he could get home to bed for a day's kip before starting work. Chiz's place on the Stockholm to Gothenburg leg was taken by Russell Ritchie, a bit of a comedown from the previous evening's limo. Psycho Sid and big Davie Lewis shared the driving. A large mouse that had swollen up under Sid's left eye, a legacy of some playful wrestling with big Davie, proved to be no impediment when behind the wheel.

The City Hotel was our base in Gothenburg. A reasonably priced joint by Swedish standards and conveniently located just off of the Avenue, the city's main street for restaurants and pubs. The camper van was abandoned directly in front of the hotel to collect more parking tickets. Once again, the hotel room proved to be a handy left luggage compartment. And, once again, we set off to find a pub called the Dubliner where a reunion which harked back to '92 was taking place. It was beginning to feel like the bloody Dubliner was following us around.

Four Fingers had business to attend to in Gothenburg. Somewhere along the way he had lost his passport and was concerned about being able to get out of the country and back into Denmark to pick up his flight home. After acquiring a very long police report which mentioned a stolen bag and listed its contents: passport, top of the range camera, good suit, full highland dress (hired), two pairs of new shoes, … and cuddly toy, a visit was made to the British Consulate.

We finally located the Consulate, a small first floor office in the busy Nordstan indoor shopping centre. A lady's voice told us over the intercom that she was very hungry. The morning had been extremely busy and the staff were looking forward to their lunch. She buzzed us up after an impassioned appeal to her humanity. It turned out that Four Fingers wouldn't need a passport to get out of Denmark and into Sweden. His problem, we were told, might be getting into Britain. Well that was one worry out of the way.

The Consulate chap who was dealing with us was a politely spoken Englishman. A nice bloke it seemed. I noticed a Scottish football pennant hanging on the wall.

'Yes, we all enjoyed the Scottish fans' visit in 1992. Not one arrest you know?'

'Yes, we got an award for good behaviour, you know,' I replied.

'Yes, pity all British, oh sorry English, fans can't behave. There was some trouble last week on the ferry over, you know.'

'No, I didn't know, what happened?'

Apparently seventeen of our southerly neighbours travelling on the Harwich – Gothenburg ferry en route to Oslo for England's friendly against Norway had been a little high spirited. A few beers, some aggro, helped themselves to free drinks then smashed up the bar, thus complicating things for all the other passengers. Unfortunately for them there was a coach load of Tartan Army on the same ferry. Grigor's mob. The press had called it a riot, but according to the Consulate official that was stretching what was a mere skirmish. Regrettably one woman had been injured and broke her leg. We later discovered that it was Moira Brown, a stalwart of the Tartan Army. She had slipped in a pool of vomit and broke her leg in three places. Some 'British' people just can't hold their drink.

On arriving in Gothenburg our southerly neighbours were deported, but the ferry company refused to carry them back. The Consulate intervened and organised a special deal with British Airways. The polite civil servant was extremely pleased with the deal he'd managed to set up: tickets at around one-third the normal price. I told him that this information was very useful as there probably would be a lot of Scottish fans also looking for assistance to get home. (I was thinking about Billy Dunn at the time).

'Do you think I look like Mel Gibson from this angle?' Freedom!! (In Gothenburg.)

'Should we just tell folk to come to the office and ask for you then?' At this point the civil servant was overcome with hunger, informed us that our call would be recorded as 'two fans in need of help', and quickly retired for his lunch.

'Two fans in need of help,' muttered Four Fingers as we descended the stairs. 'That's a good one. There's a few hundred of us in this country in need of help, psychiatric help, and they're all in kilts.'

Predictably, one fan who ended up needing assistance was Billy Dunn from Pittenweem. As we discovered in an earlier chapter, when it comes to missing your flight, train, boat or coach home, Billy is a serial offender. On this occasion Billy conspired to miss five consecutive flights home, was befriended by a Swedish family in Gothenburg and was spotted making his way down to the docks in the company of navy personnel. Apparently there was a British naval frigate in town and Billy was of a mind to hitch a lift. This plan did not work out. A

Billy Dunn: serial passport loser. A photo no immigration officer has ever seen.

week later Billy was still around, having made firm friends with a group of IFK Gothenburg fans. They took him to a match in the 'old' Ullevi Stadium, which is next to the new one but a good deal smaller. The game was against Stockholm and generated some crowd trouble. There was Billy, skint but quite happy, a solitary figure still in the kilt, caught up in a street skirmish between IFK and Stockholm fans. He was only trying to get home. Billy's record for failing to get home when apparently making serious efforts to try and do so stands at thirteen days.

Russell Ritchie and Psycho Sid paid a visit to the new Ullevi Stadium on the Friday. It was pleasant to browse through the sporting hall of fame. The walls are adorned with photos of Sweden's sporting heroes past and present. As they moved into the café area at the end of the museum they spotted Johnny Marr's nose. This appeared in a photograph of Tartan Army from '92. It was a shot from the rear showing only the backs of people's heads. Well everyone was facing forward except for Johnny who was caught glancing sideways in case he was missing something. Not wishing to be unkind, but it's rumoured that Steve Martin modelled his beak on Johnny's nose for his role in the film *Roxanne*. The café turned out to be full of photos of the Scotland fans from the Euro finals.

The camper van party was reduced to four for the final leg of the journey from Gothenburg to Malmo. Our concern about losing a large part of the £300 deposit due to damage proved groundless. The van cleaned up okay and passed the inspection. But we lost a large part of the deposit due to some of the parking tickets we had collected on our travels. The Stockholm police had phoned the hire company. The van had attracted their attention, as well as a wad of tickets, during its period of abandonment in a Stockholm side street. The police had phoned to inquire if the van had been stolen and alerted Mr Rassmussen to the matter of the parking fines. So we were hit for a handful of tickets, but still salvaged a few quid.

At least we got it back still in working order, which is more that can be said about one fan I'd been having a laugh with back in the Dubliner. This bloke had hired a van to drive to Italy in

'I'd rather stay up here than spend a night in that stinking camper van.'

1990. As they begun to descend from the Alps into northern Italy they stopped to enjoy the scenery. The view from on high was stunning and they were not the only vehicle which had stopped in admiration. A plush Mercedes had pulled in further down the hill and the driver was outside taking pictures. He was oblivious as the van, the handbreak not having been properly applied, began to roll forward. It was the noise which caught his attention as the

Merc's driver's door, which had been left open, was ripped off by the runaway van before it careered off the road.

It was probably just as well our campaign in Sweden was coming to an end. There were some worrying signs that some members of our depleted party were losing it. There was, for example, the incident of Four Fingers and the talking lift. This occurred in the Residents Hotel in Malmo, a plush abode where we spent our second last night. At breakfast Tam announced that he was spooked by the lift. He could hear it talking to him.

'Don't be daft, the lift doesn't talk,' said Auld Davie.

'Ah tell you it does. Bet it does. Go and see for yersel.' So Auld Davie gets up from his breakfast to go up and down in the lift. The journey passed in silence. But Four Fingers was certain and waved over a waiter.

'Look will you tell these people about the lift. It talks, doesn't it.' A compassionate look, a gentle smile and a slow shake of the waiter's head:

'No sir, you are mistaken. The lift does not speak.'

Mind you, it took another day, but Auld Davie was starting to show some queer traits himself. Back in Copenhagen on our final evening he was found in a pub, sitting at a table with two very large and very colourful African females from the Masai tribe. Very strange things were going on at that table, and under it, when Four Fingers and myself joined them.

The conversation which followed was interesting as we learned a bit about each others' culture.

'So how do you become a chief in your tribe?' inquired Tam.

'You must kill someone who commands respect' replied the Masai whose arms were all over Auld Davie.

'Oh, I see. Like who?'

'Like him,' she said looking straight at the auld yin who all of a sudden was looking very uncomfortable and ready to go. We did leave shortly after that, with the two Masai, and accompanied them to an event organised by the African community. Once inside it wasn't just Auld Davie who was on edge, so our stay was brief.

The next morning Auld Davie was seen in less threatening female company. This time the lady was in a cardboard box, very deflated, and on her way home as a present for Willie Scott, a retired train driver and a drinking companion of Auld Davie's from the Vale Bar next to Glasgow's Queen Street Station. Willie Scott has since been enlisted in the Tartan Army and we will meet him later in the book.

So it was all over bar the shouting. The shouting took place at Copenhagen Airport as Four Fingers lost the place after being told that he could not get on the plane without a passport. Coming at the end of an exhausting campaign this was not what Tam wanted to hear. Starting off firm and logical, and as pleasant as he could be, he pointed out that it should not be their problem.

'Surely it's for the authorities in Manchester to convince themselves that I'm not an unwelcome alien!' Okay, it was an unfortunate choice of words. One glance at Four Fingers and that's precisely what you might think he is.

Anyway, for whatever reason, he got no change out of the airline officials and stormed off in despair:

'Would someone please fucking help me.' We could hear him entering the airport bar. So after a little help from his friends they accepted his luggage and he was gone. Perhaps it is appropriate to let Four Fingers round off this tale with a little poem he put together during a quiet night on the taxis in Stockport. After all, despite what he says, the camper van was his idea in the first place.

My name is Thomas Ritchie
And the story I will tell
Is of seven Tartan Army
And the Camper Van from Hell

We all met up in Denmark
Just tae have a beer
How we all got over there
It isnae very clear

There wiz Chizzy, me, McArthur
Johnny Marr as well
Big Davie and the Auld Yin
And Psycho Sid his sel

We went oot tae a night club
Just tae hiv mer beer
Then a guy behind us said
'Hello there are ye queer'

I tried to grab McArthur
As you might understand
But a guy that looked like a wumin
Hid 'um by the hand

I said to him 'we're leaving'
He said 'you're free to pass'
I think McArthur fancied him
His hand wiz on his ass

We left that club behind us
And we hadn't got that far
When me and Mad McArthur
Had found another bar

Well me and Mad McArthur
Stayed out all night long
When we went back in the morning
The other five had gone

We raced down to the harbour
To try and catch the boat
Suddenly it dawned on me
That I had lost my coat

Inside there was my passport
And other things as well
I thought I wouldn't make it
To the 'Camper Van from Hell'

But we made it across the watter
A don't know we just did
But waiting there to meet us
Were Chiz 'n' Psycho Sid

We all set out for Malmo
Our party seven strong
We hid only gist arrived
When it started tae go wrong

Big Davie wis the driver
At his side was Psycho Sid
Marr kept falling over
And the Auld Yin flipped his lid

The Auld Yin didnae like it
When we broke the cupboard door
Then ah heard him roarin'
'I can't take any more'

On arrival in Norkopping
We nearly ditched the van
You should have seen the Auld Yin
I'm sure he even ran

We started out as seven
Now we're down tae three
The other four had left us
Chizzy, Marr and me

The three they left behind
Were soon the three no more
When Marr came back wi' Timmy the Dog
We became 'The Famous Four'

Now we're here in Stockholm
There's none of us that's well
I think the best solution
Is tae find a nice hotel

The room that we booked into
Wiz only meant fur three
Bit when I woke in the morning
There wiz three on tap ae me

We started feeling better
In fact we felt quite fine
'Til Sid came back tae tell us
That they'd got a parking fine

Now its tae the Football
Fur that is why we're here
Apart from Mad McArthur
He only wanted beer

We got into a limo
McArthur and myself
It cost a bloody fortune
Bit whit the bloody hell

We all went into Sloppies
To swally some mer beer
There also were some women there
But some of them were queer

We hid only gist arrived there
When we came face to face
With a girl that had a sauna
Back at her mother's place

I heard her say to Johnny
My place is not so near
But three of you are welcome
For a sauna and a beer

We all went with this lassie
Including Johnny Marr
I don't think we'd have bothered
If we'd known it wiz that far

We travelled there by taxi
Twenty miles or more
Johnny paid with plastic
As I got out the door

THE CAMPER VAN FROM HELL

Now we're in the sauna
Johnny, Jim and me
Jim he had a hard on
For everyone tae see

Then into a sex shop
But first intae a bank
And that mad bastard Chizzy
Paid eight pounds for a wank

Eight pounds is not expensive
That I know fine well
But what he really paid for
Wiz to have a wank his sel

He went into the booth
With tissue in his fist
And waited for the show to start
Before he used his wrist

Wanking is my forte
But you might not agree
Unlike go'n out shaggin
You cannae catch VD

Now we're off tae Gothenburg
Tae drop off Johnny Marr
Chizzy's still in Stockholm
In the Dublin Irish Bar

We're going tae hiv an easy night
At least that's what I think
But Johnny hiz a new idea
We're all back on the drink

So now it's back tae Malmo
Tae dump the Camper Van
'N me and Mad McArthur
Will clean it best we can

The Auld Yin and Big Davie
Went oot fur a beer
Bit the bar man said tae them baith
Ye cannae come in here

And now it's back tae Denmark
We'll hiv to take it slow
All of us are skint now
But then ye'll never know

No sooner had we got there
We went oot fur a beer
We went into the 'Spunk Bar'
I thought the name was queer

The credit cards got hammered
On that long last night
As for Mad McArthur
I'm sure that man's nae right

We could blame it on McArthur
I think we might as well
It wiz he who made the booking
For the Camper Van from Hell

So now it's tae the airport
We've got tae catch the plane
I've no got a passport
I hope I make it hame

The story's nearly over
But there's something I will add
The trip we had tae Sweden
It wisnae aw that bad

If one day we return there
I think we might as well
There's one thing that we won't be in
The 'Camper Van for Hell'

(A poem by Tam Ritchie aged 5)

CHAPTER 5

FREE TAM RITCHIE:
A STEREOTYPICAL PORTRAIT OF A
FOOTSOLDIER ON MANOUVRES

TAM (FOUR FINGERS) RITCHIE ENJOYED his short pre-Euro '96 visit to the USA for the friendly game against America. Just as well, as Four Fingers won't be going back there for a wee while. It was funny to see Tam's mug fill the TV screen from Trafalgar Square a few weeks later when it appeared on the national news the Friday before the England game at Wembley. An amusing sight at the best of times, but all the more so on this occasion in the light of his conversation with an interviewer asking if he thought there would be any trouble during the championships.

'No, not from these lads,' insisted Tam looking proudly towards the crowd in full flow around him. 'I've been all round the world with these boys and I can honestly say I have never seen any trouble. If there's any problems they certainly won't come from us.' Tam was spot on, but he should have added that sometimes there is the odd exception, like himself.

Tam's pride at what had just passed earlier that morning, when a party of Tartan Army paid their respects to Wallace by laying a floral wreath at the plaque dedicated to the great patriot near London's Smithfield market, had understandably shortened his memory and erased, albeit temporarily, the disturbing and hilarious events in Hartford, Connecticut, on the weekend of 25/26 May. Understanding is not what flooded into Tam's wife's mind when she eventually found out about his troubles in Hartford, or to be more precise, the consequences of those troubles.

Tam's wife Audrey loves her annual vacation in the States, preferring Florida over most of the other locations she and Tam have visited. Returning to Florida, or to any other part of the good old USA for that matter, with her hubby in tow for any length of time could prove to be problematic. To say Tam would not be welcomed back to the States with open arms is not quite right. The problem for Four Fingers is that the welcoming arms will be the long arms of the law.

A sizable contingent of the Tartan Army planning to attend the friendly against the USA based themselves for a couple of days in Hartford, a small city of around 200,000 people. Hartford's economy has been declining, but of more immediate concern for the local residents was the prospect of a race riot following the shooting to death of a black gang leader only days before. This small detail was of no interest to the Tartan Army which descended on the few pubs and nightclubs available with an exuberance bordering on the innocent, or reckless, depending on your point of view.

The local police were not oblivious to the growing tension in the town and were becoming more and more nervous by the day. Four Fingers soon found out that this was not a good time to upset them. He spotted a police car, its engine running but no cops inside. They weren't far away, just in a shop nearby for cigarettes or something, and came back to find Tam in the driver's seat, on the police radio and in full voice giving it *Flower of Scotland*. Tam did not know it at the time, but every squad car in Hartford, along with police central control, had the pleasure of hearing him. *Flower of Scotland* may not have been their cup of tea, but, as Tam was giving his rendition on the emergency channel, no other radio traffic could clog up the air waves. Had a bank been robbed or an officer gone down, there would have been nothing else for it, the polis would just have had to bide their time until Tam had finished his wee turn.

Tam had been cuffed and was being helped into the back of the vehicle when Johnny Marr emerged from Coaches pub. Johnny's efforts to assist were firmly rebuffed and he was left under no illusion that if he failed to remove himself pronto he'd

'Four Fingers' re-enacts resisting arrest.

be filling the remaining seat in rear of the car. At the same time Tam, reluctant to accompany the police, was informed that if he refused to get both legs inside they would be broken. That was the last thing Four Fingers, a man who was medically retired from a career in the post office at 27, needed. The last Johnny saw of him that evening was a forlorn face, with the hint of a tear in the eye and mouthing a silent 'help me' through the closed back window of the police vehicle as it pulled away.

Many of us didn't find out about Tam's incarceration until we turned up at the game the following day. This was being played in a tiny place called New Britain, about 15 miles from Hartford and as dead a joint as you could imagine. As for the ground, it was little more than a public park with what looked like a couple of temporary stands erected along each side of the pitch. There was a fair amount of banter taking place outside the ground among small groups of Scots fans and representatives of 'Sam's Army'. In the weeks leading up to the game the computer literate could have enjoyed some dialogue on the 'information super highway' (the Internet) between fans of the two countries. Arrangements had been made to share a few beers before the game in the time honoured American tradition of 'tailgating': scooping up at the boot of your car.

It was here that more people found out about Tam's plight. Johnny Marr takes the credit for organising a series of makeshift tee-shirts sporting a variety of campaigning slogans like: *The Stockport one is innocent* and *Free Tam Ritchie*. The information spread like wildfire: long faces all round. The Tartan Army would be handicapped. We were without our own favourite quasimodo.

But it was even worse than this. We were also denied the

opportunity of raising our glasses in toast to our absent friend. The game was totally dry. Despite the heat and the gala day atmosphere, the many stalls, without exception, disappointed, catering only for those with a liking for coke, hot dogs and Hershey bars. Sympathy for the detained one dwindled when it was suggested that he may have had inside information about the catering plans and had conspired to get himself lifted in order to miss the game. Sympathy evaporated altogether as we watched Scotland, after a good start, going down 2:1 to the USA.

It was a strange sight indeed to see Auld Davie King fumbling through his wallet to pull out a few dollars in exchange for a couple of cokes. It was more surprising when, in the process of doing so, I noticed that he was clutching two British passports. He looked equally surprised when I said 'hey, what are you doing with two passports?' He'd no idea. A closer inspection identified one of the two belonged to big Davie Lewis. By sheer coincidence big Davie was just a few folk behind in the queue for 'drinks.' Though unaware that it had left his possession, he was greatly cheered when his passport was returned, and was just as baffled as the rest of us as to how it had found its way into Auld Davie's stewardship in the first place.

There were in fact no reports of lost passports during the Tartan Army's time in the USA. Quite an astonishing statistic given the state that many of the footsoldiers got themselves into

'Four Fingers' enjoys a taste of liberty, equality and fraternity. (Not to mention lager.)

and in the light of past performances. As you might have guessed by now, the British passport is one of the items most commonly lost when the Tartan Army is on manoeuvers, though whether a Scottish passport would stand any better chance of surviving a foreign campaign is debatable.

While the intrepid Billy Dunn is without doubt the premier guru of passport losers, a growing band of would-be pretenders populate the second division. Four Fingers squeezed into this category himself during the trawl around Sweden in October 1995 in the Camper Van from Hell. He failed to work himself up the divisional ladder during his five days in the USA, but, although he managed to retain his passport, he must be commended for losing everything else, including his liberty for 25 hours.

It was the back of 9pm on the Sunday evening when a steel door at the side of Hartford Police Headquarters eventually swung open and the solitary figure emerged. I was waiting with a local shopkeeper from Hartford who had shut up early for the night and drove me out to collect Tam. She had been a great help in handling the later stages of the negotiations with the police. The lady certainly knew the ropes. Her experience had been acquired through previous dealings with the local constabulary. She had, on one particular occasion, shot a robber in the face during a botched hold up of her store.

The fortuitous link with this lady was made when I had asked to use her phone. Young John Smith, who runs the Vale Bar in Glasgow and who was on his first tour of duty, had orchestrated a frenzy of hedonism next door in Coaches: a great juke box, bodies jumping everywhere, jugs of beer all round, verbal abuse of local skinheads and a girl called Hazel from Hackney wearing a Scotland top and an old guy's hat and entertaining people in the tiny toilet at the end of the bar. The mayhem made it impossible to telephone from inside the pub.

The two of us were standing about 50 yards away as Four Fingers emerged from the police station. Even in the dusk of the evening he looked a forlorn figure. Slip on shoes, no socks, thin pale legs, a hired kilt complete with cigarette burn, a sporran, no belt, and a yellow London Scottish tee-shirt stretched taught around his swollen belly. Undaunted, Tam strode a few steps towards us, raised his head followed by right arm and clenched fist and cried 'FREEDOM.'

Back in Coaches, in between accommodating requests for *Flower of Scotland* and Elvis' *Jailhouse Rock*, Tam recounted tales from his spell in the cell. It had taken him hours to establish exactly where he was and why he was there. Things had become clearer by the time he met with the City's Bail Commissioner, although by this time Tam's memory recall had been active for fully 23 hours.

A kiss from Quasi…

'Do you have any problems with drugs?' 'Do you have any problems with alcohol?' These were among the questions put to him and to which Tam replied in the negative. 'And do you know why you were arrested?' asked the Commissioner.

'Yes,' replied Tam, 'I was steamin' drunk.' John Barleycorn was most certainly involved in the events of the previous evening, as he often is. But, as the arresting officer had explained to myself and Auld Davie when we went to the station after the game, Tam was facing not one, but around five charges. These included giving the wrong name.

Our first two hours in the police station that afternoon had been very confusing. The police were unable to confirm that Tam had even been lifted. They had no trace of a Tam Ritchie, although they had booked a Thomas Crilley for a disturbance uncannily close to the one we described. We later discovered that Crilley is Tam's middle name, he simply forgot to give them his last.

'If he has given us a false name that is bad for him. It will probably add another $500 dollars to his bail which will already be around $500,' advised a friendly desk officer. When the arresting officer eventually arrived to see us another complication arose which threw doubt on Tam's whereabouts.

'This friend of yours, what is his date of birth?' We couldn't say exactly, but we knew Tam was around 35. 'Oh no,' replied the cop, 'the man I booked last night was much older than that.' 'Well he's had a hard life you see,' I offered, now convinced that we were talking about the same person.

The bail question preoccupied a few of the less inebriated Tartan Army when Auld Davie and myself eventually got back to town after spending several hours at police headquarters. We left the cop shop at about 5pm, having been advised to telephone in a couple of hours for an update. We hadn't seen Tam. He was still being held 'up town' in Lafayette Street but was to be transported to Headquarters soon. At that time things did not look good. The police could not see him being released as he was probably to appear in court on Tuesday, Monday (the next day) being a holiday. Tam was due to fly back with us to Manchester from JFK on Monday evening. However, if released, the police forecast bail at between $500 to $1,000, depending on how the Bail Commissioner viewed the confusion over his identity.

It was obvious we could do no more for the time being. We were also parched. So we set off to report back and consider our next move. The city rose in front of us but after walking for half an hour alongside a busy freeway it was getting no closer. A phone at a grubby motel found us a taxi and we got back to town that day.

A police van had passed us by when we were walking, going in the opposite direction. We waved, just in case Tam was in transit. He told us later he was, in the back with a couple of black prisoners, and saw us through a slit in the side of the van. In fact all the fellow detainees Tam came across were black. One inmate across the corridor had hung himself. Tam didn't see much, but heard the commotion as officers tried unsuccessfully to revive him.

Some of us suspected Four Fingers may, indirectly, have had a hand in the tragedy. Excessive talking when his fellow inmate was in a fragile emotional state was a popular theory. To say that Tam finds it hard not to talk is an understatement. If denied human interaction for any length of time, he's on the phone, either from home or on the mobile if he's in his taxi. If you ever find yourself in Tam's cab it will pay you to talk. At the very least look interested in his Tartan Army tales. Fares have a habit of creeping up or down depending on the level of interest the passenger shows in Tam's conversation. Also, avoid being cheeky when asking advice on the best pubs to go to. These customers are usually dropped off at a gay bar.

Tam recalls one particular passenger he was sorry to see the back of. An air hostess he picked up from Manchester Airport in the wee small hours of Monday 22 April 1996. Tam began to prattle on excitedly about the coming Scotland trip to the USA and was delighted to find his passenger had a keen interest in the Tartan Army.

'So you lads will all know each other then,' the stewardess asked.

'Sure,' says Tam, 'there's a core group of fans and we try and get to as many away games as we can. Friendlies, the lot.'

'You wouldn't happen to know a John Marr, would you?', she asked.

'Johnny Marr! Of course, I just saw him a few days ago. He came down to Blackpool for the Easter weekend with a troop of girls and a haggis and organised a Burns' supper in one of the pubs. So you know Johnny. Oh, I could tell you some stories about him.'

'Don't bother,' the lady cut in, 'just tell me how I can get hold of him.' Four Fingers was now more than a little curious.

'No problem, I can help you there,' as he dialled Marr's number on his mobile and passed it to the stewardess.

It was a worthwhile move. 'You're the crazy bastard that caused all the trouble on the flight to Rimini last year,' was the first thing Johnny heard after lifting his bedside phone at 2.30am and confirming that he was, indeed, Mr John Marr. 'All that commotion you caused at the front of the plane was out of order. I had a new girl with me on that flight. She was just trained. It was her first flight. You loonies wrecked her head and she handed in her notice after that flight. We tried to tell her that it had never been like that before, but she still left.'

As you would understand, coming out of a deep sleep, it took Johnny a few moments to get his historical bearings and log on to the particular flight in question. Crazy behaviour high in the sky was not, in itself, a terribly helpful clue. It was not a simple task for Johnny to grasp what journey this obviously very pissed off lady was ranting on about. But he got it eventually.

'Hold on a minute dear, I don't know what your talking about. I was sitting at the back of the plane and couldn't really see what was going on up front for the folk dancing in the middle.' Four Fingers tells us he enjoyed the situation so much that he let her off with the fare. Now that's a tall story!

During the Euro Championships a few of us based ourselves in Stockport, dividing ourselves between Tam's and big Davie's gaffs. Here we had the opportunity to observe Four Fingers' normal habits at first hand. The man is a gem, but he's also a serial phone caller. A phonophile, whose telephone bills each quarter look as though you've got a kid who has been secretly calling chat line numbers on a daily basis for a year. I recall the misfortune of sharing a room with Tam in Estonia. I was going to settle the total bill by Visa so Tam squared me up for four nights in cash. At the desk I queried the size of the bill. Surely it couldn't be that much? The confusion was quickly dispelled when the receptionist drew my attention to the computer output of charges. This ran to nearly three pages. The first two inches dealt with the room rate. The rest was taken up by 'Telephone'.

Back in the USA, although it was only a fraction of Tam's annual phone bill, there was no obvious way that we could raise the level of bail we expected the Hartford Bail Commissioner to set. Between us we could muster a few hundred bucks, but nowhere near the expected grand. For the time being liquid resources were sorely depleted and, as it was Sunday evening, banks could not be hit with credit cards. We were not confident that the Commissioner would accept credit either. As for travellers cheques, these are virtually an unknown item among the hard core Tartan Army.

Thankfully, the final call to the cops from the angel who ran the shop next door to Coaches brought the news that Tam was being released. Not only that, but no bail was being demanded up front. He was out on a PTA, a 'Promise to Appear,' and had given an undertaking to appear at court on the Tuesday. However, by then he was safely tucked up in bed back in Stockport after having had to wake up his next door neighbour for keys. His own keys were in his travel bag which was lying somewhere back in New York.

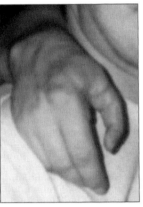

The offending paw....

Tam's identity wasn't the only confusion for the cops. Finger printing the felon proved another stumbling block. The process involved inking each finger of the right hand in turn, then inserting the print in one of the five boxes on the card, starting with the pinkie, each box on the card being marked to take the print of a particular finger. So far so good with the first three fingers. But when the cop came to the fourth he realised that this was the last on offer and he still had two boxes to fill. This fourth and final finger was where this guy's thumb ought to be, but this was no thumb. It looked more like a pinkie!

The cop was correct on both counts, but the fingerprint card was well and truly screwed up and he was more than a bit bewildered. He may have been interested to know the background to his immediate dilemma. A few years before, Tam had lost a chunk of his right hand, including his thumb, in a lift accident. The surgeon patched him up pretty good though he had to be a bit creative in the process. This involved removing the pinkie of his hand and sewing it on where the thumb used to be.

By the time Tam and the rest of the Tartan Army had negotiated their way up to Connecticut, the Big Apple had been well and truly tasted. Some of the troops had been in New York for the best part of a week, like the lads from Yell in Shetland who returned to Carney, New Jersey, with warm memories of the hospitality they had received in the Scots Club when they were in the States, and Scotland weren't, for the World Cup in '94. For others based in Manhattan, Annie Moors pub directly across from Grand Central Station was the meeting place and the Vanderbilt YMCA was base camp.

The Rod Stewart concert at Madison Square Garden on the Thursday before the game drew a few of the troops from Annie Moors and culminated with Rod and the Scottish team giving a rousing rendition of *Purple Heather*. But by this time a number of the Tartan Army had already left, not through choice, because Rod was giving a fine performance, but due to some of the stewards taking exception to the degree of audience participation being demonstrated by people in kilts.

Anyway, at least Rod did not leave empty handed. He was fortunate enough to acquire Gus Clark's Saltire from big Dave Lewis. He couldn't avoid it. It hit him smack in the face as he ascended up through a trap door

A Neil Aitken look-a-like...

on the stage. The flag ended up pictured in the Daily Record, draped around Rod and the Scotland team. Prior to this, big Davie lost his kiltpin and bust his watch spracklin' with six bouncers in the lead up to his premature departure from the concert. Davie was not alone. About half a dozen of us who had ventured into the Garden were back at the bar in Annie Moors well before *Purple Heather*.

It was not all boozin' it up in Manhattan. The Tartan Army took time to take in well known sights like Harlem, the Bronx and Central Park after dark. In fact, in the wee small hours following Rod's concert, big Davie took advantage of the fine weather and dossed down in Central Park. He had a reasonable kip, disturbed only once by a mugger. The would be mugger was a bit taken aback when big Davie, dressed in great highland plaid, stood up, booted him and chased him into the bushes.

Wee Geordie and Danny Divers, returning from an eventful night in Harlem and enjoying an early morning stroll in Central

Park, came across big Davie who, on waking, proceeded to perform a highland jig on top of a wall. The dance was abruptly interrupted when a weird looking woman appeared from behind a bush screaming 'get down, get down, the birds will starve.' Davie was tramping on bits of bread she had put out for the birds, but not for long. To the woman's horror the food was swiftly gathered up and devoured.

The trio were soon in the company of some of Central Park's regulars, sharing refreshments from brown paper bags. The party attracted the attention of other itinerants. One guy was selling small bags of sweets. He tried to engage Wee Geordie in some trade.

'I am hungry. I need a few dollars to buy something to eat.' Geordie was an unfortunate choice, being probably nearly as skint as the tramp was, and not perhaps the most sympathetic of the group.

'Well if you're hungry, eat your sweets,' Geordie suggested, trying to be as helpful as he could.

Another character met with more success. He presented himself as an ethnic American Indian who was trying to get back west to his reservation to visit a seriously ill relative. His plight struck a chord with Wee Geordie who insisted on collecting a fistful of notes from the others. The Indian's eyes widened with delight. 'Thank you very, very much. Are you guys Irish?' At which point Geordie's outstretched hand snatched back the notes. He was unimpressed by the apparent failure of the Indian to distinguish between the diverse cultures of the Celtic fringe. Geordie's short philanthropic career was brought to an abrupt end.

Pan handlers would have been well advised to turn up the following morning at the Hyatt Hotel where Wee Geordie, Young John, Danny Divers, Four Fingers, and myself were killing time and deciding how to get ourselves up

Chairty begins at the squat.

to Hartford. An attempt to secure coffee and bagels at a stall in the hotel foyer failed when the stall keeper suddenly downed tools and walked off with no explanation, leaving one of our party standing empty-handed at the stall. While waiting for him to return a Japanese couple came up and asked for coffee and cookies. The couple went away happy, a little confused, but with their faith in human nature strengthened after being served and told that as it was Saturday 'there would be no charge for coffee and cookies today.' Several other couples were accommodated in a similar way before the Tartan waiter walked off the job just before the stall keeper returned to resume his post.

Several modes of transport were employed to get the Tartan Army northwards to Connecticut. Auld Davie and his pal Willie Scott (on his first campaign) took the train. Willie, whose last route as a train driver with British Rail was the Glasgow-Aberdeen service, felt right at home. The train broke down.

'It's a buckage fault,' announced Willie, 'all they need to do is release some air and we'll be away in no time.' His advice was acted upon by one of the passengers, apparently a regular on the route.

'Well done,' called a female guard, 'thank you for your help. Have a nice day.'

Train travel did not appeal to Marr's group from the Edinburgh Tartan Army who arranged for a fleet of white stretch limousines to spirit themselves northwards to Hartford. The limo option was rejected by the five of us in the Hyatt Hotel. Instead, we decided on a helicopter, and one was booked to pick us up at the East River. A price of $1,666 dollars was quoted but after some dogged negotiation we managed to beat the price down to $1,660. It took only 45 minutes to fly to Hartford, although to Young John and Tam, who discovered that the concept of helicopter travel was more appealing than the reality and who shook and sweated for the whole flight, the trip seemed a lot longer.

It took us another four hours to prise ourselves out of the small bar in Hartford Airport. A group of construction workers, already pished when we arrived, joined the party at the airport

and decided to enlist in the Tartan Army for the rest of the day.
Our new friends were good enough to drive us into the city.
Young John, Danny Divers and myself travelled standing in the
back of a speeding, Ford V8 pickup truck, flags flying and singing:

We're comin', we're comin',
Were comin' down the road,
When you hear the noise
Of the Tartan Army Boys,
We're comin' down the road.

We repeated the chant over and over again like mantras to take
our minds off what was a near death experience. It was a relief
when the truck finally stopped at the Sheraton Hotel, but not
before crashing over the traffic island just in front of the main
entrance, finally coming to a halt a few feet from the window. At
the other side of the window were officials and players from the
Scotland squad, the Sheraton being the team's hotel in Hartford.
'Oh no, they're here.' It was obvious from some of the expressions
that Tartan Army were the last characters they wanted to see.

Six of us departed Hartford on Monday with the fugitive Four
Fingers in tow. Not by helicopter this time, but by Peter Pan Bus;
inappropriately named as we had all aged about five years over the
past few days. The bus pulled out and made its way along the
appropriately named Asylum Street. Back in Papa's 24 hour café
we had just bade farewell to a number of our fellow loonies with
time on their hands and plans to make the Colombia game in
Miami on the Wednesday. Johnny Marr was trying to whip up
support for his idea of visiting the Niagara Falls while Psycho Sid,
who had never really recovered from the Camper Van from Hell,
was twitching and muttering

'That's it Johnny, never again, never again,' as the sweat dripped
onto his plate of scrambled eggs and bacon. Johnny's mob didn't
make the Miami match (a 1:0 defeat). They got back to New York
City, booked flights to Florida, missed them, and spent the rest of
the week stoatin' around Manhattan.

Those we left behind enjoyed mixed fortunes during their

remaining time in the US. Wee Geordie, for instance, had no intention of staying on until the Wednesday but nearly did after losing his flight ticket home. He was disgusted that such a common occurrence could cause so much hassle. The airline was insisting that he buy a new ticket. This was out of the question. The British Consulate proved equally unhelpful. But that was before Wee Geordie informed them that he was skint and had no wish to remain in the USA any longer than necessary. If they could not help him then he would have no alternative but to beg and camp out on the stairs of their building. One look at Wee Geordie and the Consulate quickly concluded that this was not a prospect to relish. A call to the United Airlines quickly sorted out another ticket.

Big Davie left Hartford to spend a day in Boston followed by a day at the beach before travelling back to New York in search of stragglers from the Edinburgh Tartan Army and the London Scottish. In the process he came across a couple of stunners, Joan and Leslie, who were more than happy to show him around Greenwich Village. The body language was just right and Davie was feeling good.

'You Scotsmen are so shy. You can touch us too you know,' teased Joan. By this time Davie was more than feeling good.

'Look David, put your hand down here.' As Leslie steered Davie's hand, he found out that the slacks were not a 'hers', they were a 'his'.

'What's the problem?' pleaded Joan, as Davie beat a hasty retreat.

Big Davie should not be too dismayed. Others have found themselves in stickier situations than this. One of the Tartan Army in Tallinn thought he had cracked it with what he believed to be an American female weightlifter. The two of them left Hell's Hunt for a bit of casual fun in a nearby park. Things were fine when the American's head was behind his sporran, but...

Meantime in another part of Manhattan, Stef of the London Scottish, who earns his corn as a member of the Metropolitan Police, relieved Johnny Marr as social organiser and was trying to find a suitable bar in the Chelsea area. Stef, whose nickname in the Met is Gurkha because he takes no prisoners, is one of the tidier dressers among the footsoldiers, with tweed kilt jacket, polished shoes, clean shirt and tie. A tactical strategy designed, with some success, to attract girls away from other Tartan Army when they begin to fall apart at the seams. On this occasion Stef chose badly and led the group into a basement disco reminiscent of the heavy leather and chains joints in the Al Pacino film *Cruising*. The kilts proved an immediate attraction. Before the troops could regroup and flee, professional looking photographers with lighting equipment were on the scene.

'Right Stef, we're out of here now,' insisted Schillachi, 'before we end up in the next edition of *Gay Weekly.*'

They didn't stay long in the next bar either. It looked safe, but pretty dead. A small jazz band jamming and a smattering of customers chatting quietly over drinks. The boys looked around, about turned and left. They got no more than 30 yards when a trumpet sounded behind them It was the band leader out on the pavement starting a rendition of *Loch Lomond*. Back in the bar the trumpeter played *Loch Lomond* another four times before the night was out. Here Johnny got talking to the Russian-born manager of Macabi Haifa, an Israeli football team. Johnny explained that he was once a top footballer who would have made a big impact on the world stage had his career not been prematurely ended by a crippling knee injury. The pair agreed that Johnny would scout for Macabi Haifa in the UK for a fee to be negotiated at a later date. And some people still wonder why Johnny has a long nose?

It is coincidental, but only a month before, Greg Kain and Ian Clarkson of the Partick Thistle International Supporters Section were involved in a similar jest when in Copenhagen for the friendly against Denmark. They got chatting to a couple of Polish students in the Dubliner, one of whom turned out to be a semi-professional footballer, understandably keen for a move abroad. Posing as scouts for Partick Thistle, Greg and Ian proceeded to arrange a trial date and negotiated a provisional salary and signing on fee. They assume he must have been a fairly tidy player, because the next morning they were visited by a journalist from a Danish national newspaper asking for further details on their signing plans. Sure enough, the interview was published in the paper the next day.

Back again in New York City, Stef managed to redeem himself a bit the following day. With the group sleeping and missing their Miami flight, what was left of the day was spent in Manhattan. Wall Street and Battery Park were visited before Schillachi declared 'Fuck this, let's get back to the Village and check out a place that plays Bob Dylan.' The boys noticed Stef approach an NYPD van and engage an officer in conversation.

A few minutes later he called over 'c'mon boys we're onto a lift.' Into the back they piled, and with the siren on made the Village a hellava lot quicker than they would have on the underground. Stef had flashed his ID and pointed out that a fellow police officer could use some assistance.

Four Fingers made it back to Manchester, but his troubles were not far behind. As Willie Scott says, Tam is an accident waiting to happen, and you don't have to wait around to long. Tam loves a wee bet on the horses. But the bookie might as well tear up the slip before he gives him it. Everything he touches turns to shit. Even small things get screwed up. Like when he asked Willie and Auld Davie what they wanted for dinner when they stayed with him during Euro '96. Mince and tatties was the order. Tam goes shopping and comes back without the mince.

But the letter he received in September 1996 was more serious than missing mince. It was headed *United States of America Extradition and Warrant Service*. It was from the Central Office of the Criminal Prosecutor and read as follows:

Mr Ritchie, we have been informed by our prosecution service that you failed to appear in Connecticut Central Court in relation to several offenses that took place in Hartford Connecticut on Sunday 26 May, 1996.
I write to notify you that I am hereby commencing formal proceedings with HM Government of the United Kingdom Foreign Office to have an extradition order placed. Should I not hear from you by 14 October, 1996 I shall instruct our lawyers to proceed accordingly.

I must stress that it is in your interest to treat this matter seriously and respond by return in order that the current position can be clarified.

This letter does not infringe your civil rights as a citizen of the United Kingdom. You will, however, be fully committed to the laws governing the United States of America should the extradition order be carried through.

Tam was on the phone to me ten minutes after he had signed for the receipt of the letter.

'Someone's winding you up,' was my first response. 'Check the post mark on the envelope and see where it's from. That'll soon tell you if it's genuine or not.' The envelope said it had been posted in Washington DC. 'Surely they wouldn't go to all that trouble for a joke,' I said as the letter began to grow in authenticity in Tam's mind. He was looking for advice. 'Look, why don't you phone Stef. He's a cop. He might not know much about extradition orders, but at least he should be able to find out where you stand,' I suggested.

I left a very worried Tam to act on this advice. Half an hour later the phone went again.

'It's that bastard Marr,' laughed Four Fingers. Johnny had done well getting a friend to post the letter when he was over in the States, but he'd slipped up on one small detail. The letter had been printed on a sheet of paper which, when held up to the light, exposed the name of Johnny's employer as a watermark. Four Fingers had slipped off the hook.

CHAPTER 6

JIMMY HILL IS, WILLIAM WALLACE ISNAE

THE JIMMY HILL ANTHEM HIT THE AIRWAVES after Scotland's unsuccessful tilt at England during Euro '96. Chris Evans, then a Radio 1 DJ, had met a group of Scots and had been so impressed by the classic verse that he sang it the very next day. Euro '96 had been the first time in nine years that the Jimmy Hill song had been sung by a choir of thousands on English soil. During that period Wembley's star had begun to wane as the Tartan Army marched beyond the shores of Britain. Indeed, for many of the younger Scots fans, the game against England was their first Wembley. Apart from the younger first time fans, Wembley '96 was probably the smallest turnout by the Scots support against England in living memory.

But let's not delude ourselves. Scotland against the auld enemy still commands a place in the heart and threatens to generate a huge Scottish turnout. It always has. Shortly before the regular biennial fixture was stopped indefinitely, who can forget the large banner raised among the thousands of Scottish fans one wet Wednesday night. A midweek date had been specially selected to make absolutely sure that Scots, certainly in any significant number, would not beat the FA's ban on tickets finding their way north of the border. The banner read: 'So you thought you could ban us from Wembley Mr Croker?' A message of defiance to the then Secretary of the Football Association. I wonder if it was the same punters who raised the 'Alcoholism v Communism' banner at the Scotland v Russia game in Spain 1982?

The Tartan Army has recast its image since the Wembley

fixture was stopped. Almost without exception, Scots fans get rave reviews wherever they go these days. You just need only to look at the coverage in the local papers. In fact, a lot of the troops buy the papers and bring them home. As mementoes? Maybe. As atonement for past (and possibly) future indiscretions? Who can tell. Yet, even today, there are folk back home who are unconvinced by the new, squeaky clean image. You get people who smile wryly and nod heads with a 'give it time' knowing look when enthusiasts eulogise about the ambassadorial qualities of the Tartan Army. As we will see in a later chapter, even sections of our own press are uncomfortable with the Tartan Army's recent PR.

Are the doubters justified? Long memories are not required to recall England's national stadium being systematically taken apart in 1977 after Scotland's great 2:1 victory. Many of today's regular foreign legion were there and, heaven forbid, were no innocent bystanders. Yours truly got his bit of turf from just where big Gordon McQueen began his run to nod Bonnie Scotland's second goal. I'd just been chatting with a policewoman who was finding it difficult to hold a conversation because on the other side of her a guy in a tartan tammy and scarf was giving a policehorse a drink out of his can of beer.

But Wembley was different. Sure the Scots in London were no angels. We never were. I am grateful to a former colleague, Bert Moorhouse (a Tottenham Hotspur fan), for the following two press reports. They are from some years ago, but still read pretty fresh. The first is from 1949 (which also happened to be Auld Davie's first Wembley):

> Thousands of deliriously happy fans bedecked in tartan scarves and tam o' shanters, with rattles, bells, bagpipes, thronged London last night celebrating Scotland's win over England in the international championship. It was London's most vivid and colourful celebration and Piccadilly Circus, Coventry Street, and Trafalgar Square were solid with people. The Circus had to be closed to traffic. A police guard was put around Eros in case some too enthusiastic Scots climbed the statue. Hundreds of visitors went driving. They blew horns, waved flags, sat on the roofs and windows of the buses. Diners in restaurants in evening dress, gathered at the balconies to watch as groups of Scots sang

national airs... One miniature army of Scots carried swords fashioned out of sticks as it marched along Regent Street. (*Sunday Express*, 10 April 1949)

The other piece, an extract from the *Daily Record* in 1930, referring to an assault on Wembley when thousands without tickets rushed the stadium, continues:

Some even went as far as to remove earth and concrete from under the railings, and, in this way caused a breach through which they could pass....Fortunately, however, the timely intervention of foot and mounted police reduced the danger of thousands flocking into the already crowded enclosure. (*Daily Record*, 7 April 1930)

For the weekend of the match on 15 June '96 Trafalgar Square, once again, performed its traditional role as host to a massive party. Saturday's celebrations were disrupted a bit by English hooligans, but the Friday was almost just like old times. However, there was some serious business to attend to before we were able to join the festivities. About thirty Tartan Army assembled at St. Paul's underground station at 11am. Our piper struck up and from there the group made its way to the square facing Smithfield

From 1296 to Euro '96, the spirit of William Wallace lives on.

Market. On the opposite side of the square from the market, indented into a wall of the former St. Bartholomew's Hospital, is a memorial plaque. It commemorates Scotland's great patriot, Sir William Wallace, who was cruelly executed nearby at Smithfield Elms on August 23, 1305. Under a rampant lion shield it reads:

TO THE IMMORTAL MEMORY OF

SIR WILLIAM WALLACE

SCOTTISH PATRIOT BORN AT ELDERSLIE
RENFREWSHIRE CIRCA 1270 AND WHO FROM
THE YEAR 1296 FOUGHT DAUNTLESSLY
IN DEFENCE OF HIS COUNTRY'S LIBERTY AND
INDEPENDENCE IN THE FACE OF FEARFUL
ODDS AND GREAT HARDSHIP BEING
EVENTUALLY BETRAYED AND CAPTURED
BROUGHT TO LONDON AND PUT TO DEATH
NEAR THIS SPOT ON THE
23 AUGUST 1305
HIS EXAMPLE HEROISM AND DEVOTION
INSPIRED THOSE WHO CAME AFTER HIM
TO WIN VICTORY FROM DEFEAT AND HIS
MEMORY REMAINS FOR ALL TIME A SOURCE
OF PRIDE HONOUR AND INSPIRATION
TO HIS COUNTRYMEN

It then continues in Latin: DICO TIBI VERUM LIBERTAS OPTIMA RERUMNUNQUAM SERVILI SUB NEXU VIVITO FILI. This translates into: 'To tell you the truth, liberty is the best of things. Son, never live under a servile yolk.' Below that there is a final message: BAS AGUS BUAIDH These Gaelic words translate as: 'Death and Victory.'

Johnny Marr had been charged with the arranging of a commemoration wreath. This he did, but received an earful from some of the more discriminating footsoldiers because it was a wreath of red, not white, roses as is the tradition of Jacobites. Wee Geordie did well in delivering a speech on behalf of Scotland and the Tartan Army. Johnny Marr laid the wreath. Auld Davie hauled his 71 year old body up onto a ledge in front of the mass of assembled press and, with clenched fist, exclaimed 'We arra peepull.' Press cameras clicked.

Wallace, in cardboard form and bearing an uncanny resemblance to Mel Gibson, was waiting in person at Trafalgar Square to greet us. He had travelled down with a party of Tartan Army from the Vale of Leven, whose

Flowers for a national hero. (At least he never missed a penalty against England.)

local team were at one time champions of the world, but which is now better known to many as a neighbouring settlement to Dumbarton. Wallace looked happy to get a break from standing in the corner of the Global Video rental shop in the Vale where he had spent the last couple of months. Our piper, Sean McGloinan, born in the South Bronx, New York, piped us through the streets of London to the Square. The march took about an hour, allowing for three refreshment stops on the way.

At Trafalgar Square it was the same old routine: unremitting singing from the central stage, football in the pools although the fountains had been switched off, huge carry oots, and friendly banter with the polis. Even at 71 years, Auld Davie King managed up onto the back of one of the lions at the foot of Nelson's Column. The Scots' performance was widely appreciated by the tourists. One American woman interviewed on the national news had come to London to see Buckingham Palace and the other well known tourist attractions. She had intended spending the Friday at the museums but told the cameras: 'This is incredible. This is much more fun. Who are these guys?'

The behaviour of the Scottish supporters before, during and after matches was later recognised by Birmingham City Council. Scotland had played two games in Birmingham during Euro '96, against Holland (0:0) and Switzerland (a 1:0 victory). After the

Championships were over, the City Council sent a small delegation to Glasgow to present the SFA's president, Bill Dickie, with a scroll commending the Tartan Army for 'outstanding conduct and friendliness.'

However, although in the words of the SFA 'the supporters' magnificent behaviour merited accolades from the police and the local communities,' not everyone was happy with the Tartan Army. A Birmingham bar owner was interviewed by the press about trouble from fans. Pressed repeatedly to comment on what problems the Scots fans had caused he eventually conceded that there had, in fact, been one problem after all. The vultures' pens and pads sprung to the ready in anticipation of juicy detail. The problem occurred, he explained, when the fans went to the game and his pub was empty for a couple of hours. Frank Sinatra had a point when he called the press just 'bums and hookers'.

Euro '96 was yet another chance for Scots and Dutch fans to develop their already warm relationship. Fifteen Dutch, wearing kilts and Holland tops, distributed small pairs of clogs as souvenirs to the Tartan Army in Birmingham pubs while 500 Scots and Dutch fans assembled at the campsite and marched into the city centre behind a piper. Local office workers watched in amazement as Scots and Dutch fans, linked arm and arm, waved and sang: 'What's it like to be at work? What's it like to be at work?'

The Dutch proved to be more than able singing partners. They had no difficulty with most of the songs although they did lose it a bit when it came to the Jimmy Hill anthem. This problem could potentially affect many nationalities and threatens to inhibit the further development

A Birmingham Pub 'riot'. Missed by the media.

Wallace – liberated from a video shop – goes sight-seeing at Trafalgar Square.

of joint singing and mutual understanding between nations. Thankfully, shortly after Euro '96 the problem was in the process of being rectified. A Tartan Army Home Page appeared on the Internet sporting a 'We Hate Jimmy Hill' Page. This served an important educational function by aspiring to translate the famous song into as many languages as possible.

Congratulations are in order for professional translator Tam McTurk, who thought up the idea for this hugely useful section of the Tartan Army Home Page. The inspiration came to him a couple of days before the Wembley match when he found himself in a restaurant with a number of Italians and Ukranians. Tam was trying to explain the concept of the famous chant and its origins from the World Cup in 1982 when Jimmy had described David Narey's glorious opening goal against Brazil in Seville as a 'toe poke'. By the end of the evening the company was singing the verse in seven different languages.

Greatly encouraged by this success, and over a few beers prior to the Wembley match, Tam and two fellow footsoldiers were giving further thought as to how other foreigners could be introduced to the famous anthem in future. It was during this discussion that a flash of inspiration came. They would develop a set of translations which would help Scots anywhere in the world who found themselves in a similar predicament to Tam and place these on the Internet.

Boosted by DJ Chris Evans' unexpected plug, the Jimmy Hill song attracted a healthy degree of media attention. But a backlash was building up. One of the first dissenters to the lyrical sentiments expressed was a certain Mrs Hill who was not at all impressed. The day following the Radio 1 airing of

'I know a nice wee sauna in Sweden; you bring the handcuffs, babe.'

the anthem, the tabloid press reported Mrs Hill as saying that since Jimmy has had two previous wives, and between the three of them has sired five children, then this was significant evidence that the song was incorrect.

The third Mrs Hill has a point, but does this mean that the 20,000 Scots at the Sweden game in Genoa in 1990, and the countless thousands of others who have concurred at Scotland games and many other events over the years, are misguided? Was the

Hello Jimmy.

Scottish newspaper *Scotland on Sunday* also off the mark when it suggested Mr Hill should appear '*IN THE DOCK*' and face the following charge:

James Hill, you are charged with monumental wind-baggery, discrediting the admirable name of ****s and generally getting up humanity's nose with your unctuous sermonising and verbal keech.

If you wish to read the full piece, the original article, containing the case for the prosecution and a thoroughly unconvincing, and ultimately unsuccessful, case for the defence is reproduced below.

In the Dock No 14... Jimmy Hill

THE CHARGE

James Hill, you are charged with monumental windbaggery, discrediting the admirable name of ****s and generally getting up humanity's nose with your unctuous sermonising and verbal keech.

THE PROSECUTION

They say the best way to deal with arrogance is to let it exhaust itself. But, like the proverbial fart in a phone-booth, Mr Hill and his infinite reservoir of sanctimonious tripe have lingered in our midst for what must be an eternity.

He first came to the attention of the Scottish public in the 1960s and soon emerged as a serious contender for Alf Ramsey in the most-pompous-English-twat stakes. Admittedly, in the days when the likes of Dickie Davies and Archie Macpherson were being heralded as heavyweight TV pundits, it could be argued that absolutely anyone could attain a degree of media eminence merely by having a microphone shoved in their vicinity. And it certainly fooled the Arabs. Hill was summoned to Riyadh in 1976 to oversee the restructuring of the game in Saudi and, 13 years later, Scotland got a glimpse of his legacy as we took on the Saudis in the World Youth Tournament Final at Hampden Park: the visiting youngsters all sported Jimmy Hill beards as birth certificates were intensively perused amid a climate of suspicion and disbelief.

But it was on a balmy Seville evening in 1982 that the man's rampant Scotophobia finally surfaced in all its malignant glory as David Narey's wonderful strike against Brazil was dismissed as a "toe-poke". The Jimmy Hill Abatement Society gathered ground and his sexual orientation was remorselessly questioned by the fuming Tartan hoardes. Rumours that Hill had joined the Village People remain sadly unproven.

If any prospective civilisation ever gets around to recreating an identikit image of a figure who effortlessly managed to rile the Scot during the latter half of the 20th century, it shall contain the following components: a bloated ego, condescension by the mouthful delivered in a status in football inversely proportionate to actual talent and a signature bearing the words... Jimmy Bloody Hill.

CASE FOR THE DEFENCE

Counsel for the accused have repeatedly alluded to Hill's involvement in the abolition of the maximum wage in 1961 while chairman of the English PFA, and the improvement in the professional footballer's lot thereafter, as evidence of his benign influence on the game. But frankly, this court feels he has been dining out on these events for the past 35 years and they shall conveniently be ignored in the interest of satisfying our craving to see the obnoxious git adequately chastised.

VERDICT

Not since Alan Rough was discovered trafficking in stolen mince has the burden of guilt been so overwhelmingly established. The jury are appalled at your antics Mr Hill, and appropriate retribution must be swiftly and painfully exacted. You shall be led from these chambers, muzzled in the interests of curtailing noise pollution, and paraded in front of a baying crowd at Hampden Park where you shall be the victim of a public bechinning. Take him down.

Raymond Travers

It is worth noting that that Jimmy's alleged infamy extends well beyond the Tartan Army. For instance, I had the pleasure of meeting some Pittsburgh Steelers fans in the summer of '97 when I was over in the US for a wedding. It cropped up in conversation that I followed Scotland abroad whereupon this guy Baldric asked me if I was familiar with.....Yes, they had already been introduced to the Jimmy Hill song by a Scot they had met and loved it, but maintained there was no-one of Jimmy's persuasion in Pittsburgh. They were also pleased to say that they had done their bit to popularise the verse in Florida when the Steelers had played the Miami Dolphins in the Orange Bowl Stadium, and Baldric had orchestrated the group singing. A few hundred hard core Pittsburgh Steelers fans now know all about Jimmy Hill, and many more fans who attended the match at the Orange Bowl left asking 'Who the hell is this guy Jimmy Hill?'

Even so, in the face of such overwhelming opinion, dissenting voices have been raised. Some, for example, have been aired through the Internet. A great advantage of this technology is that it gives people from all corners of the globe the opportunity to communicate with each other. Anyone connected to the Internet can enjoy the Tartan Army Home Pages and engage in a discussion with others using it. It is perhaps inevitable that such open technology will attract people who, whether for reasons of culture, humour or whatever, are unable to grasp the essence of what's really going on. The following contribution to the Discussion Board of the Tartan Army Home Page was received from a certain Paul J. Walsh:

> I am writing to you in response to your Tartan Army Home Page and in particular your page concerning Jimmy Hill. Firstly, would you not find it more constructive to dedicate a page to a player from a Scottish football team? I cannot fully understand why someone would take the time to promote hatred towards a particular person and group which your home page has shown. Would it not be more effective if you expressed your content with your footie team and the Tartan Army, rather than show all who visit your page your ignorance towards others? Are you seeking tolerance, acceptance and recognition of Scottish football from the BBC and Jimmy Hill? Do these means help in any way?

As for Jimmy Hill's a **** chant, I also can't quite understand how calling someone a **** is meant to be an insult. Is calling a Scottish person a Scot an insult? Is calling a straight person a straight an insult? Please note: heterosexuality isn't normal, just common. Please try a new politically correct chant as your cause benefits no-one. Thank you for taking the time to read this and I hope to hear of a positive and encouraging response.

Mr Walsh clearly misses the point and has, unfortunately, acquired a dim view of the Tartan Army. His hope for a 'positive response' would not have been served by another contribution to the Discussion Board, this time from a Steven McGowan who had just been to the Switzerland game in Birmingham:

> Having never been to a Scotland game before I didn't know what to expect. I wasn't disappointed. The atmosphere in and around the stadium was just amazing and to gaze across at the upper tier of the Holte End almost brought tears to see so many of my fellow countrymen chanting about Jimmy Hill. The whole experience of being amongst the Tartan Army was breathtaking.

Nice one, Cyrillic: Mr Hill's fame as a football pundit spreads even as far as Russia.

Mr McGowan was obviously quite happy, but complaints about the Jimmy Hill section continued and provoked the following response from the computer literate footsoldier who set up the Tartan Army Home Pages and published the contributions people sent in:

Please don't bother sending complaints about this page. If you don't like it then don't read it. It is simply a chant to show our united dislike of the man, his attitude and his chin. Please note the page is not intended to insult or show disrespect to anyone from the gay community - the word **** is known to be 'politically incorrect' but there is not much can be done to change the chant now!

Sadly, I have to report that the Tartan Army Home Page had its website sponsorship from the brewer giant Scottish Courage withdrawn. The soccer commentator reportedly lost the rag when he logged onto the Tartan Army Home Page. The following article (by correspondent John Arlidge) appeared in *The Observer* newspaper on 11 May 1997 (page 4) and gives a good account of the dispute.

Jimmy Hill is used to taking insults on the chin. The veteran football commentator has been the butt of terrace jibes since he first appeared on *Match of the Day* 25 years ago. But now, goaded by his oldest foes, the long-suffering pundit has finally lost his sense of humour.

Hill, 68, is so angry at disparaging comments made by Scottish football fans on the Internet that he is suing the brewer Scottish Courage, official sponsor of the Tartan Army website. Hill, chairman of Fulham, is loathed in Scotland for his criticism of the national team, and is demanding substantial damages and a full public apology.

When the Edinburgh-based brewer recently agreed to sponsor the website, it offered virtual reality fans free cans of lager and boasted that the site could teach them to sing 'We hate Jimmy Hill, He's a ****, he's a ****!' in more than 30 languages.

The Tartan Army needed little encouragement. So many supporters logged onto the site - described as the 'good natured face of Scottish football' - that the publishers soon set up an official 'We Hate Jimmy Hill Page.' On it, fans ridiculed Hill's 'comical appearance', condemned his playing career a 'crap' and his commentaries as 'shite', and described him as an 'English bastard'. Some referred to him in the 'trousers department'.

Worse, a competition began to translate the famous terrace chant, 'We hate Jimmy Hill, he's a ****, he's a ****!' into 32 languages. It was a huge success. One Hill-hater from China even e-mailed a Mandarin version: 'Women bu siquan Jimmy Hill, Ta shi yigi *****, Ta shi yigi *****.' Zulu and Serbo-Croat translations also appeared.

When he saw it, the normally unflappable Hill was not amused. After consulting his lawyers, he wrote to Scottish Courage, Britain's biggest brewer, demanding a full public apology and 'substantial' compensation.

He said: 'It is difficult to understand how a company of your reputation could authorise and condone the publication of crude, offensive and highly defamatory material.' He went on to accuse Courage of cynically exploiting fans' worst instincts simply to sell more lager. Hill himself has declined requests for interviews but David Roodyn, his solicitor, told *The Observer*: 'Jimmy Hill is a courteous, understanding man who accepts laddish behaviour and banter in good spirits. He likes Scottish people although he is aware that he is not popular with some Scottish football fans. He is outraged that a big brewer like Scottish Courage is fomenting hatred against him just because it wants to boost profits. Jimmy Hill is a very important figure in post-war football and he is very upset.'

A spokeswoman for Scottish Courage said that the firm was proud of its links with the 'peaceful, pleasant' Tartan Army. It was 'unfortunate' that Hill had been offended and any obscene material would be removed from the Internet. But she went on: 'The website is a forum for members of the Tartan Army to air their views; the views are the fans' views and we neither condemn nor condone.'

Mr Roodyn replied: 'If a company sponsors a website it has a duty to show that it is acting reasonably and what is published is within the law. Scottish Courage's own remarks of an obscene sexual nature are defamatory and its attempts to encourage fans to make further defamatory comments by translating a crude song are quite unreasonable.

One final, uplifting point to make before leaving the demise of the Jimmy Hill Page is that, before the axe fell, the target of 32 languages had not only been reached, but exceeded. Surfers of the Web were able to enjoy the song in a total of 36 different languages.

The joke is now over and Jimmy Hill received an undisclosed out of court settlement and an official apology from Scottish Courage. The page disappeared from the Internet and the publicity died away. The whole episode remains as yet another of those well trodden Tartan Army stories which will form the basis for hazy discussion in the years to come.

The writer would like to make it clear, for the avoidance of doubt, that the contents of the foregoing chapter concerning James Hill, the football commentator, are a description of the relationship between Mr Hill and the supporters of the Scotland Football Team. Nothing contained herein should be construed as imputing anything about James Hill, his personality, his reputation and in particular his sexuality. The author would like to state his profound respect for Mr Hill and his reputation as a football pundit, notwithstanding his disagreement with Mr Hill's analysis of a goal scored by Scotland in the 1982 World Cup Finals.

CHAPTER 7

A BOOT IN THE BALTICS

JULIE ANDREWS, TYROLLEAN MOUNTAIN MEADOWS and happy Von Trapp children were what used to come to mind when I heard *Doe a Deer*. But that was before October '96. When the *Sound of Music* was first doing its rounds in the former Gaumount cinema in Sauchiehall Street back in the 60s, Julie Andrews and the Von Trapp family entertained the Glasgow public during a run of many months. After Scotland's history making Baltic campaign for the planned double header against Latvia and its neighbour to the north, Estonia, Julie's song will never be the same. Latvian police and public stood bewildered as the crowd of around 1,000 Scottish fans in the Daugava Stadium sang *Doe a Deer* over and over again during Scotland's fine 2:0 victory. Even folk watching on the TV back home and more familiar with the madcap antics of the Tartan Army wondered what the hell was going on. By the time we reached Tallinn the song had been learned by heart and the handful of Estonians in the Kadriorg Stadium were treated to an example of group singing that would have been the envy of every Von Trapp.

Regrettably Mr. A. Lamb from Edinburgh did not participate in the singing. A. Lamb was one of a group of seven of us who had booked flights with SAS through Trailfinders in Glasgow. But at the last minute his work decided his services were required in Qatar; duties which had to take priority over the Baltic campaign. Despite the substantial custom SAS had enjoyed from Scottish fans in the past, the airline refused to allow a change of name on A. Lamb's ticket. 'So what can be done?' we asked at their office.

'Well, what you can do,' they suggested, 'is to cancel the ticket. There is a waiting list you see. The seat can then go to the next person on the list.' 'So will Mr. Lamb get his money back?' 'Well, no,' explained the SAS representative, 'but it means that we will be able to sell the seat again to someone else.'

Unable to follow the logic of this advice, we decided that if A. Lamb could not go then 'a lamb' should take his place. An old passport was duly found, an inflatable sheep which had last seen active service in the Faroe Islands was conscripted from the bottom of Johnny Marr's wardrobe and the necessary passport-sized photograph was taken. In the absence of A. Lamb, the plan was to take his namesake to the airport and present it along with doctored passport and valid flight ticket at the SAS check-in desk for through travel from Glasgow to Riga via Copenhagen with the rest of us. In the event the lamb did not travel. At the last minute SAS relented and agreed that the ticket could be reissued to someone else joining our group. This was Martin Riddell, another Edinburgh Tartan Army member. The charge? Payment again in full.

When the Tartan Army trooped home around a week later there were others in tow which raised a few eyebrows. One, who by this time had won a space in all of our hearts, was a 12 foot long snake with a head larger than big Colin MacDonald's, a member of the Edinburgh Tartan Army and a native of Ballachulish, who was part of our band for the Baltic trip. The snake had joined us in Riga, shortly after we had met up with a large bear liberated from probably the most expensive toy shop in the city.

The bear was extremely popular but got carried away with all the excitement. He was last seen on the Friday night, rather the worse for wear, in Klub 3 with a long line of untouched drinks and in the company of two young ladies. The ladies were showering the bear with affection and he was lapping it up.

The Riga Bear. Lucky bastard.

Unknown to him, one of the Tartan Army had weighed the girls in with a generous wad of Lats (the national currency) with the request that they 'take care of the bear and be sure to tend to his every wish.' I guess they did. He did not return to the Hotel Riga. A search party led by Gus Clark and Colin MacDonald was formed the next day, but the bear remained AWOL. His service with the Tartan Army had been brief but happy. If any reader ever gets the chance to see Prendy's video memoirs of Riga you will not miss the sight of a five foot bear in full swing in Paddy Whelan's Irish bar.

The snake went the distance and travelled back home with our party. By the time it got back to Scotland it had been to two World Cup qualifying games, one of which did not happen, passed through a total of five countries in the space of a week, drunk copious amounts of alcohol, including a memorable vodka frenzy in the company of Russian Mafia, learned the words of *Doe a Deer* and almost spent a night in the same room as Tam 'Four Fingers' Ritchie.

By the way, if you are ever thinking of sleeping in the vicinity of Four Fingers don't bother, because you can't, not unless you're stone deaf. There is no rhythm or pattern to the sounds he makes. But there is plenty of noise. If you do find yourself in this tricky spot you could follow the example of his mates when they turned up back at their room in the Hotel Sport in Tallinn and found, to their horror, the deformed one past his best. 'No way he's staying in here,' proclaimed Marr. No sooner had he got the words out than big Colin scooped Tam up, carried him out of the room and deposited the naked body in the corridor. When Tam awoke later, he was staring up at three hotel gun totting security guards. 'What are you doing here?,' one of them demanded. 'You tell me,' said the bewildered Tam, 'I haven't got a clue. What floor am I on anyway?'

Thanks to his pals the snake did not have to put up with Four Fingers. However, the journey back to Scotland via Finland and England was not a pleasant one for the reptile. The airport staff at Tallinn insisted in winding him into a huge ball, binding him with sticky tape and lodging him in the hold. We could see our friend being loaded and unloaded from the window of the plane, which was reassuring, but looked painful all the same. But the snake made it safely back to Auld Reekie, began to settle in to his new home in Johnny Marr's flat in Gorgie and became the first snake to be officially enrolled as a member of the Edinburgh Tartan Army. His friends were even planning to apply for membership of the SFA Travel Club and had sent for the necessary forms.

The Riga Snake: now on tour in the Nimeta Bar, Tallinn, Estonia. Completely hissed again.

Sadly the snake's story does not end happily. For the Saturday night before the 'backs against the wall' 1:0 victory against Sweden at Ibrox on Sunday 10 November, 1996, the Edinburgh Tartan Army arranged a get together, booking the second floor of the Rock Café in Princes Street. The night was a great success. The Peterhead Crew, the Shetland boys and some of the London Scottish contingent made it as did many others including Russell Ritchie, sister Pamela and Kevin Lewis from Fife. Neil Aitken, 'Joiner and Glazier' from Coldstream, also came up with a squad of pals to celebrate his 40th.

But the snake did not appear in the Rock Café. Marr, who had managed to get a ticket for the reptile for the rugby friendly against Australia that afternoon, had foolishly left his friend in the company of big Davie Lewis and Danny McGovern. Danny had been a splendid host during the European Championships when he threw open the Vine Bar which he ran in London's Kentish Town; the only hostelry in central London offering free accommodation to the Scots fans. But neither Danny nor big Davie were top of Johnny's Xmas card list on the Saturday night. The snake had slipped from their company whilst in Reilly's pub in the Grassmarket and had disappeared. It had either decided that it had had enough of Scotland and made a break for it, or it had been spirited away by a new 'owner'. Marr was inconsolable.

Four Fingers did make it to the get together in the Rock Café and arrived with wife Audrey. He was the centre of attention when the proceedings paused for a few minutes to accommodate a presentation to Tam.

*'It's so f***in' easy!'*
Billy Dodd's three seconds of glory in Tallinn.

The lovely Anneli Törblom, who met some of the Tartan Army for the first time in Helsinki and is now living in Edinburgh, engaged to Craig 'Shaky' Steven and doing a degree in photography, has captured quite a lot of the Tartan Army's foreign antics through the lens of her camera. One priceless shot is of Tam's goal in 'the game that never was'. The presentation to Four Fingers was a framed black and white photograph of the goal scorer lashing the ball home from the 8 yard box.

Many present in the Rock Café at that point would have been thinking back to that bizarre occasion and the days in the Baltics surrounding it.

'There's only one team in Tallinn/One team in Tallinn...'; 'Play in the daylight/We only play in the daylight...' And not forgetting the classic 'Doe a deer, a female deer...' These songs had resounded around the small stadium, empty except for around 600 Tartan Army and a few others including some of the Estonian Army which had been drafted in to assist, possibly because the stadium stewards were not there. We had watched the Scottish team play it by the book. They took to the field of play, shook hands with Mr Miroslav Radoman (the referee), kicked off, surged forward a few feet, stopped and walked back off the pitch after only three seconds of open play waving to the fans who were now singing 'We're gonna celebrate, we're gonna celebrate...'

This was Tam's cue for a solo invasion of the pitch. But first a little more background to the incident is appropriate.

A few minutes before kick off Tam had approached Mr Willie

McDougall to thank him for being so understanding in the aftermath of his misfortune in Hartford, Connecticut, a few months before. Mr McDougall, the SFA's security advisor (who replaced Mr McLaren), had phoned Tam prior to the Euro '96 Championships after a worried Tam had called the SFA to enquire why he hadn't yet got his tickets. The SFA administrator who took Tam's call said they'd get back to him.

Tam lifted his phone. 'Hello Mr. Ritchie, it's Willie McDougall here. I want to speak to you about your behaviour in Hartford, Connecticut which resulted in your incarceration.' 'Yeh, sure,' replied Tam, on the verge informing the caller to tell whoever had set him up for this to go and get stuffed. And Tam had a pretty good idea who would be behind it. But something, maybe an inherent survival instinct, for he's survived a lot, counselled caution. 'Listen, I'm not sure who you are, you could be anybody. I bet Marr's got something to do with this. I'll call you back and check you are who you say you are.' Tam did and found he was back speaking to Mr McDougall who informed him that better conduct was expected and that this rebuke should be taken as a 'warning shot across your bows!'

'Hello, Mr McDougall, I'm Tam Ritchie. We've spoke on the phone. Sorry about that problem in America,' said Tam to Willie

'Gaun Tam! Shoot!' The Tartan Army roars its support as the deformed one bears down on the Estonian goal.

when they met face to face for the first time in the Kadriorg stadium. 'Oh, so you're Thomas Ritchie,' replied Willie looking the miscreant up and down. 'It was a one off. Just one of these daft things that happens, but it won't happen again,' Tam assured him.

Maybe he should have kept a lower profile. For only five minutes later there was Tam, leading a solo charge onto the pitch with a ball at his feet, a can of McEwans Export in his right hand, and an Estonian security guard in hot pursuit. He's heading full tilt for the goals to the left with the fans roaring their encouragement.

It looked as though the pursuer was going to catch him, but as he got to the 8 yard box Tam let fly. The Tartan Army were one up and Anneli had a great photograph.

Four Fingers received the Tartan Army's unanimous verdict as our 'man of the match'. 'One Thomas Ritchie, there's only one

Come the hour, come the man. 'Four Fingers' ensures his place in history with a mazy run and clinical finish in 'the game that never was'. All without spilling a drop.

Thomas Ritchie...' sang the fans as the Scottish team nominated Billy Dodds as their man of the match in a bid to lift the player's disappointment at the outcome of what was to have been his first senior cap. 'I might never get another cap. It feels like losing a Scottish Cup final,' Dodds mourned to the Scottish football correspondents present.

Tam's example precipitated an informal kick about, with a few Estonians joining in. One fan had a 7 foot cardboard cut out of a bikini-clad beauty advertising sun tan oil on the park. This had been acquired on route to the game from a small supermarket where our mini-bus taxi had stopped off to stock up with pallets of beer for the match. The cardboard beauty left the stadium with another group of fans and was last spotted fraternising in the Club Estoria. At the game the lady defended the goals to the right of the spectating group, but had little to do.

There was only one incident during the match which gave cause for concern. An Estonian broke away on a run from the left half of the park and had a clear route to goal. A kilted fan from Aberdeen, who had up until this point been happily watching from the sideline, responded to the call. Everyone bar the Estonian could see it coming. The gathering of momentum as he bore across to intercept the attack, the crunching tackle, only one player emerging with the ball, the other left in a motionless, crumpled heap. There was some debate among the crowd about the exact height of the tackle. Did he take him out at the waist or chest? It was hard to say, but Kevin Lewis summed up the crowd's verdict: 'THAT was definitely a penalty.' Even the Estonians in the pub agreed later that night when a recorded highlight of the incident was shown on national TV.

Rumours had been circulating from the previous evening that all was not well with the lighting at the Kadriorg Stadium. Four Fingers had been chatting with former player Alex McLeish in the Hotel Sport. 'So what's happening Alex?' Tam asked. 'We don't know,' Alex replied. 'There is a problem with the floodlights. Craig and Tommy (the team coaches) are away down to the park to try and sort it out.' 'Why, are they electricians?' asked Tam. But it was not until the next day that the news broke that the game was to be brought forward close to four hours, with a rearranged kick off time of 3pm.

They shall not pass: typical Scots defensive formation in the only game 'that was' in Tallin.

The Nimeta bar on Suur-Karja in Tallinn's old town proved to be an excellent source of pre-match intelligence. Davie Coutts from Dundee, who now owns the bar, kept his customers informed of the latest developments. Others found out about the new kick off time from  posters put up by SFA staff in other pubs and fast food outlets around the city.

Big Eck tackles a pint. Pint gets stretchered off.

The Estonians, who were informed about the new kick off time early in the morning, claimed they were unable to arrange transport to get themselves to the park on time. As was subsequently reported in *The Scotsman,* 'Estonia's weakness was essentially its lack of players of any substance. For, in a fundamentally flawed tactical move, they decided not to turn up.' The Tartan Army, a disorganised unit scattered all over Tallinn only an hour or so before kick off, managed a full turnout.

For many of us it was back to the Nimeta pub for post-match celebrations, one fan making the journey in the boot of an overcrowded taxi. Estonian fans made an appearance in the Nimeta later that evening. They had watched the Estonian team turn up at the stadium at 5.15pm, 90 minutes before the original start time, where the electronic scoreboard still announced 'Eesti-Sotimaa, kick off 18.45.' When the noisy but friendly Estonians burst into the bar their singing was immediately met and drowned by a chorus of 'Where were you at 3 o'clock, where were you at 3 o'clock...'

On the whole the Scots fans were, as usual, philosophical about the whole experience, although there were some questions being asked about the SFA's preparation for the game. 'What about all these 'fact finding' missions the officials come on?' asked big Davie Lewis. 'I'd like to know what facts they find out!,' referring to the fact that no one had noticed the fact that the power in the floodlights was barely powerful enough to read a book by.

As the post-mortems continued, which included a press conference for the Estonian sports channel in the Nimeta, I think we all had a sneaking feeling about the eventual outcome. Scotland had played it by the book, but we were not really banking on the same response from FIFA. Yet it had been FIFA, after a night of faxes flying between their offices in Zurich and their representative in Tallinn, that had decided to bring the kick off time forward. And it was FIFA's regulations for the preliminary competition for the 1998 World Cup which stipulated in article six, paragraph six that:

> If a team does not report for a match – except in cases of force majeure (extenuating circumstances) recognised by the organising committee – the team shall be considered as having lost. The match and the three points shall be awarded to their opponents with a score of 3:0.

But we suspected that there would be a further twist in the tale. And there were a few to come. After several weeks of uncertainty FIFA ruled that given the exceptional circumstances a replay was in order, in Estonia by mid-March if at all possible. By this time rumours were rife that Scotland's two main rivals in the qualifying group, Sweden and Austria, had been lobbying behind the scenes in their own interest. Concerns were expressed when it was learned that a Swede – Mr Lennart Johannsen, President of FIFA – had chaired the committee which ratified that decision.

It was a decision which provoked considerable outrage among the Scottish football public and press, not least because it meant that Scotland would now be without our captain Gary McAllister, who had picked up a second booking against Latvia. This booking meant that he would automatically miss Scotland's next game. For us this should have been the 'game that never was' when McAllister had not been included in the team. FIFA didn't agree and McAllister could not strip for the crucial home game against Sweden in November. FIFA had found the circumstances sufficiently 'exceptional' to go back on their own rules, but would not alter the consequences of that decision as far as McAllister's suspension was concerned.

Quite a few fans let Mr Johannsen know just how they felt. On the morning FIFA's decision was announced Tartan Army telephone lines were buzzing with information of Mr. Johannsen's address, telephone and fax numbers. Some fans had already been on the phone that very morning to give the Swede an earful. It was later reported that Mr Johannsen was seriously annoyed at the flood of faxes and general abuse he'd been getting from Scottish fans and suspected the SFA of complicity in the campaign against him.

One of the many faxes FIFA received from the Tartan Army was from Stuart Logan of Blackpool. Stuart chose to make his point in the form of this poem, 'Scotland in Estonia':

In Tallinn the old town, by Raekoja Plats Square,
The skirl of the pipes could be heard in the air
At Kadriorg Park, the justice was cruel
FIFA decided to change all their rules

The meeting was final with a decision agreed
Chaired by Johanssen, groups rivals, a Swede
How can they treat great fans in this way
we've seen all their placards that proclaim Fair Play!

Through Denmark and Finland and Baltic seaways
The Loyal Tartan Army had travelled for days
One week and more in Estonia they stayed
In hotels and bars they boosted the trade

Scotland in Estonia, what a strange game
Three seconds of glory and fame
We travel the World to see football played
With FIFA in charge, the price that we paid.

The FIFA orchestrated farce continued. After realising that their directive about where and when the replay should take place was impossible to fulfil, Tallinn being effectively shut down for outdoor sport due to the severe Baltic winter, FIFA again were called on to sort out a venue for the game. The Estonians had suggested Cyprus where they have a training base. The SFA protested on the grounds that the five hour flight was too far for the fans to travel. The Estonians then suggested Azerbaijan, a flight of about 9 hours to the edge of a war zone. The Tartan Army were getting interested.

FIFA met and ordered the game be played in Monaco on February 11, 1997. This time it was some of the Tartan Amy who protested. Monaco was one of the most expensive places in Europe. A week's cheap package to Cyprus would have been just dandy. But Monaco it would be. The good news was that the financial demands of the campaign would be reduced. Thanks to another benevolent FIFA ruling the Tartan Army could look forward to free tickets for the game. This would amount to a saving of about £5, the equivalent of about half a pint of beer in the Principality of Monaco. Had natural justice prevailed, FIFA would have dipped into their coffers and added a couple of '0s' to their generosity.

The whole farce left a bad taste in the mouth, but The Tartan Army's affections for Estonia run high, with may footsoldiers making return journeys out of the football season. One event during the 1996 campaign highlights the fans' great feeling for Estonia and shows that the Tartan Army have a social conscience as well as a healthy appetite for creative relaxation. Tommy Madden, who was instrumental in organising the event, is best placed to tell you about it:

In 1993 a group of us from the Partick Thistle International Section set off from Glasgow to Tallinn in a mini bus. Through England, France, Belgium, Holland, Germany, Denmark, and Sweden to the port in Stockholm where the minibus was dumped and we boarded the ferry travelling to Tallinn. That same ferry *(Estonia)* sunk two years later leaving 500 Estonians drowned and their families devastated. So we decided to raise funds for the surviving families and wee Craigie presented a cheque to the Estonian Embassy. When we returned to Tallinn in 1996 we wanted to pay our respects by visiting the new memorial, 'The Broken Line', which had been built in memory of the dead. Led by a lone piper we marched through the streets of Tallinn to where the memorial overlooks the sea and paid our tribute with flowers. The event received massive coverage in the city and the 300 fans present were fêted by the Mayor of Tallinn and other dignitaries. The swapping of souvenirs was hastily arranged and Neil Ross delivered an eloquent speech. The fans were given the freedom of the city. The Scottish press hacks knew about our plans, but chose to spend their time in the Nimeta getting pished. The British High Commissioner subsequently wrote, 'Scotland Supporters are well known for their boisterous enjoyment and with this gesture show a tremendous generosity of spirit.' (signed, Brian). A nice compliment was also forthcoming from the SFA's big Willie McDougall who publicly thanked us for our actions.

*The Broken Line: in memory of victims
of the Estonia ferry disaster, in which
500 Estonians perished.*

Many fans have developed a lasting friendship with the locals in Tallinn. During our visit in October '96 Kevin Lewis stayed with a girlfriend, Marina, who works in the Sport and who he had first met before the Finland game when several hundred fans crossed the Baltic to spend a few days in Tallinn. Kevin had been sitting by himself polishing off a bottle of champagne at the hotel reception and got talking to the girl at the desk. He arranged to take her out for dinner the next night and to bring along his pal (a fisherman who must remain nameless) for her younger sister. They all ended up back at the family home for the night. Kevin woke in the morning to a lot of shouting. The mother had found the younger sister in bed with his pal. 'Is your mother mad at the two of them being together?' Kevin asked. 'No,' replied Marina. 'My mother, she is angry because my sister is late for school.'

Kevin valued his insight into how the Estonian family lived. They'd had a hard time. Kevin was told the father was a carpenter who had been forcibly taken away by the Russians to work somewhere in the Soviet Union. Where to, the mother and daughters had no idea. They had not seen or heard from him since. Marina kept in touch with Kevin and later wrote to say she had saved up money with the intention of going to Spain, but now wanted to come to Scotland instead. So to Burntisland in the Kingdom of Fife she came and had a great time. Kevin recalls her fascination with small things and how excited she became when she discovered an elevator in an Edinburgh store. This was photographed to show her friends back home.

As before, there was a considerable amount of romancing done in the Baltics. Chiz was another footsoldier who was rekindling old relationships. His friend was a long black haired lady from Tallinn in tiger skin leotard that looked like it had been painted on. One of the Edinburgh Tartan Army found himself on diplomatic service with a posh representative from the British Consulate who 'wished her boss could see her now.' Another footsoldier ended up at a luxury pad in Riga. The man of the house was away 'on business' for a few weeks, but it was clear that this was someone whose occupation demanded some heavy duty hardware. The flat was like an arsenal. The Scot made the mistake of giving the lady a keepsake in the shape of a ring which his fiancée had given him on their engagement, an act of generosity he began to regret well before he boarded the overnight train from Riga to Tallinn.

Auld Davie had also been looking forward, lustfully, to another tilt at Tallinn, recalling his last visit when his flirtation with a reasonably good looking blond in her mid-20s had made the pages of *The Guardian*. By the time the Tartan Army arrived at the game in Helsinki, a press hack had got hold of the tale of the auld yin's success and reported it in the following way:

> Among the Tartan Army following Scotland to Helsinki for the midweek international against Finland was a 30 year old chap and his 70-year-old father. After the game the son wanted to go out with the lads, so he persuaded the old man to have a quiet night in. Later the son returned to the hotel from a good evening out to find his septuagenarian father in flagrante with a lady of the long Finnish night.

This was not quite the correct story. It was the wrong country for a start! In fact, Auld Davie and Jimmy Cormack had wined and dined the lady, although she had only eyes for the older of her suitors. This I discovered on returning to our room in the Hotel Sport to find Auld Davie snuggled up in a single bed with his girlfriend on one side and a glass of beer on the other. She was not on the game, which made her a bit of an exception among the girls floating around the Hotel Sport. But she was no Mother Theresa either.

We woke to find her gone and an old pair of jeans that fitted no one in the room lying crumpled up on the floor. Also gone was a pair of new jeans, a belt, Jimmy Cormack's plastic tommy gun and, as we were to discover a couple of days later when groping in vain around our bags, the flight tickets home. Maybe the auld yin should have just paid $50 in the first place and saved us all the hassle. He'd

Old dog, new trick: Auld Davie pulling the talent in Tallin.

learned his lesson by the return visit when he managed to tan $200 in the space of four days.

'I hope you've been taking precautions,' Davie Lewis teased him when we were having a last drink in the Nimeta on the Friday afternoon. The Auld Yin feigned surprise and his position on the matter exposed him as a poor advocate of safe sex for the elderly.

'Are you jokin'? Why would I worry about catching anything serious at my age?' cried the Auld Yin.

We had a good laugh at that and laughed again when Four Fingers offered to venture in the direction of the bar. We weren't sure he'd know where to find it. Tam spending money on a drink? He'd been getting a friendly ribbing about being miserable all week.

'Where did you get the money Tam?' we demanded. We didn't know it at the time, but he'd tapped Alan Jamieson for the dosh. Big Davie is right when he says that going for a drink with Four Fingers is like going out with a blind man: tap, tap, tap.

Tam felt that he'd fared pretty well over the course of the week and by his standards he probably had. 'Do you know something,' he said to big Davie after my group had left them to catch an earlier plane, 'this is the first trip I've been on that I've not lost anything.' Tam was conveniently forgetting Auld Davie's bunnet that he'd plucked from the auld yin's heid during the first few hours in Riga and which ended up leaving the door on an anonymous Latvian's head minutes later. But a single bunnet is small beer compared to Tam's usual accomplishments. 'Give it time Tam, you're not home yet,' was big Davie's wise and prophetic reply. Sure enough, as they were called to board the second leg of their flight home in the Amsterdam Airport Tam's face fell, 'shit, I've lost my boarding card.'

Johnny Marr was walking upright when we left Tam and big Davie in the Nimeta. This came as a shock to some of us as the Wednesday night after the game was nearly the end of him. He finished up in the Palace Hotel. One of the troops sent a round of drinks over to a group of well dressed strangers. That was the start of it. The well dressed gents were not pillars of society, legitimate society that is, and they made the boys several offers they could not refuse. One of the Mafia molls who obviously found Marr and his snake a fascinating pairing was standing too close for her own good. Sergie thrust Johnny another gill of straight vodka. 'Have these people never heard of coke?' Marr lamented two days later. Down it went, a second or two's pause and back up it came, right down the lady's fur coat.

Auld Davie found Johnny, or what was left of him, back at the Hotel Sport and took him up to his room. 'Has anyone seen Marr, surely he couldn't have got a lumber the state he was in last night,' asked Gordon 'Safe' Hands at breakfast on the Thursday morning. 'Oh he's fine. I took him up to his room last night,' said Auld Davie. Gordon, Martin Riddell and Colin MacDonald stopped eating and looked at him. 'What do you mean? He should be in our room and he's not been in all night.' A comprehensive search of the third floor after breakfast eventually located the missing Marr, comatose in a complete stranger's room.

Border controls in the former Soviet Union 'aint what they

used to be. Sure a few of the coaches travelling from Riga to Tallinn were held up for a few hours at the border and one fan was searched pretty thoroughly, so thoroughly that the border guard felt it necessary to wear a rubber glove. But there were no incarcerations such as the one which befell a Hearts fan on arriving in Estonia for Scotland's first visit back in '93. Despite the worldly wise company of Jimmy Cormack on the ferry journey from Helsinki to Tallinn, the Jambo remained ignorant of the political sensitivities of the former Soviet Union and its satellite states. He turned up wearing a kilt and a Boris Yeltsin mask. This failed to endear him to his new hosts who were just beginning to savour their freedom from Russia. A resulting spell in a cell ended only after he greased a military palm with a $5 bill.

Our small party had no problems at all. Maybe we just got lucky, but I think turning up at the border pished and in full party mode may have been a factor too. Thanks to Gordon 'Safe' Hands, transport was arranged late on the Sunday afternoon. A taxi minibus scooped up six drunks from the now nearly dry bar in the Hotel Riga, plus Gordon and Auld Davie. Davie had just returned from a tour of Riga with a local couple he'd met the night before and who were keen to show him their city. Gordon, who contributes regularly to an Australian Hibs fanzine, later described the experience as 'The rowdiest trip I've ever been on.' The ghetto blaster we had chipped in for at Glasgow Airport more than paid its dues as the minibus was transformed into a mobile ceilidh for the journey north to Estonia.

At some stage in the 6 hour drive we stopped somewhere in the middle of a forest at a small wooden bar standing all on its own. We were the only customers there. Gus Clark found Free's *All Right Now* on the juke box and, as several beers were swallowed rapid, rock and rolled with a coat stand. The chaos lasted no more than ten minutes. There was a strange look on the faces of the two bar staff as we sang 'Cheerio, cheerio, cheerio...' and boarded the minibus to continue the drive north. But it was a look the Tartan Army has seen many times before.

Parties are infectious and serious faced gun totting border guards are not immune. Maybe the Scottish music got to them or perhaps Auld Davie broke the ice when he started spinning one of the female guards around as two of us attempted a rather unconvincing limbo dance under the barrier. Meanwhile, the rest searched, with a kind of 'fuck it doesn't really matter, does it?' attitude, for missing passports. Time flies when you are having fun, but I recollect our time at the border was short and I recall seeing relieved faces from the rear window as we pulled away into the darkness.

Following in the wake of the Tartan Army's move north were a few Latvians who'd got caught up in the weekend's madness in Riga. One of them was the lady who'd acquired the engagement ring. The ring's owner was still mourning its loss on the last afternoon in the Nimeta when the good lady walked in proudly sporting the gift. A bit of smooth talking, the purchase of a new bracelet from a local jewellers and the ring was back on its rightful finger. A couple of Latvian sisters were also in tow and seemed glued to the bar in the Nimeta for several days. Back in Riga they had levered a couple of fans out of the chaos of Paddy Whelan's to join them at a rock concert by a top Russian band.

The sisters had four seats near the front of this large theatre. Too close to the front to stop one of the troops from mounting the stage prior to the band appearing, taking up position on centre stage with the microphone and, amidst a great amount of cheering, announcing, 'Good evening Latvians. I'm Andy from the Tartan Army and we come in peace. Good luck for the game tomorrow. Have a great night.'

By this time the other footsoldier was up on the stage too and was intent on giving the 2,000 or so applauding music lovers a song. After only a couple of lines it was clear to Andy that any Latvians not totally tone deaf would be doubting his claim that they had come in peace. A firm arm around his friend's shoulder led him off and no damage was done. A large fierce looking geezer, who'd been shouting and gesticulating wildly while the pair had been on stage, rushed towards them as they made their way back to their seats. Perhaps an unhappy customer? But no, the guy only wanted to share a few cans of beer with them.

Leaving Riga was not a major hardship. The city had proved

not to be as friendly a place as Tallinn for the Tartan Army. Gary Keown, the Tartan Army's correspondent for the *Sun,* wrote from personal experience to that effect. Gary had made the mistake of asking a group of strangers where he 'could get a bite to eat around here?' For this indiscretion he was beaten. A short time later, his round head looking more like a panda's than it normally does, he met another group. Gary didn't put a foot wrong this time, but to no avail. A gun was pulled and a second beating was meted out. Gary, for one, was pleased to see the back of Riga.

Neil 'Joiner and Glazier' Aitken also had a bit of scrape with a knife wielding hood and, not to be outdone, Murray 'Lucky' Frazer chipped in with another of his own misfortunes. You will probably remember 'Lucky': the Aberdeen lad who got battered by thugs and knocked down by a car in Athens a couple of days after his girlfriend had packed him in and who later got knocked back from entering Russia when he arrived at the airport in Moscow because some pen pusher at the embassy had made a mistake with the stamp on his visa. This time Lucky started early, got a kickin' in London on the way out, was hit by a bogey £250 telephone bill in his hotel in Riga and then was fined $30 on the spot by police for urinating in bushes outside the stadium. The Latvian cops were clearly beginning to get the hang of the enterprise spirit. Scots fans looking for the toilet were directed towards the bushes. Once in the bushes other cops were getting rich with 'on-the-spot' fines.

While the police were coining it in, the local taxi drivers were finding the currency consequences of having the Tartan Army in town a bit difficult. One group of the fans who hadn't quite got the hang of Lats handed a taxi driver a fistful of notes. This posed the guy some problems as he fumbled around for change. The troops were trying to tell the guy to forget it, when he ushered them to the rear of the car, opened up the boot and presented them with a large fish. The fish accompanied them around a few pubs and was last seen face down in an empty pint tumbler.

The atmosphere was certainly more relaxed in Tallinn, an atmosphere greatly enhanced by fellow fans recollecting incidents from previous visits to the city. The first visit had been back in

1993; a 2:0 victory over Estonia in a World Cup qualifier. On that occasion, Kenny (The General) Reid was sharing a few refreshments with a certain Robbie the Pict. In what at the time was the only night club in Estonia, a very rude Finn with his girlfriend in tow bumped past spilling their drinks without as much as a by-your-leave. Naturally, the lads were none too chuffed. With the Finn's attention elsewhere, a glass of vodka and orange was slipped under a kilt.

'Ah, but how do we know it was the guy's drink?' The General asked. Just to make sure, the other glass was put through the same routine.

People were surprised to see Robbie the Pict in Estonia. He is not a regular with the Tartan Army, but more importantly it was rumoured that this fanatical patriot refused to travel on a British passport and had been demanding that the Government furnish him with a Scots one. The Pict was also alleged to have refused to fork up his annual car tax on the grounds that the money goes to the London Exchequer. He is now a leading light in the fight against tolls on the Skye Bridge.

The General's next trip to Tallinn found him in the company of Ian Lawrence who had been highly impressed with the hospitality shown to Scots fans during the 1993 visit. Ian and his pal, Davie Coutts, had spotted commercial opportunities offered as this country emerged from the shadow of the Russian Bear. Ian and Davie had been looking at the possibility of buying a bar called 'Eslitaal'. They had been going over the accounts for the place and had uncovered a puzzling discrepancy. Now the Eslitaal was not what you would call a gold mine, but there was one period, over a year back, when takings appeared to go through the roof. The two of them were beginning to harbour serious doubts about the reliability of the financial data they had been presented with when they suddenly twigged. The puzzling inconsistency became glaringly obvious. The rogue week coincided with Scotland's previous World Cup visit.

In Estonian, Eslitaal means 'horse.' Near the railway station in Tallinn tourists will find plenty of horses and carts waiting to guide them around the delightful old part of the city. It was not uncommon to see Tartan Cavalry in control of the horses, with the guides sitting back relaxed in the carts. The Scots steered their charges not just through the cobbled streets of the old town, but between busy lines of city centre traffic. One of the more adventurous equestrians was spotted mounted on a horse's back.

One footsoldier had really got the hang of racing the cart through heavy traffic. The only time that the 'guide' seemed remotely concerned was when the Scot pulled up too abruptly, launching himself headlong over the front of the cart and down behind the horses hind legs. A few minor scratches were all he had to show for it. On completion of his self help tour of central Tallinn he stood both guide and horse a drink at a café near the station. The guide had a black coffee. The horse had a beer.

The Tartan Army's romance with Tallinn and Estonia continues. The city is visited regularly by Tartan Army. Chiz and Jim Black have been over for Hogmanay a couple of times. For his workers' Xmas 1997 outing, Ian Mathieson (Edinburgh born and now a successful businessman in Bristol) opted against the local restaurant and took his whole workforce of nearly twenty to Tallinn for a couple of days. Kenny McAskill, a barrister, to celebrate his 40th birthday in 1998 hired the national stadium in Tallinn to take on a local parliamentary select with an open invitation extended to the Tartan Army.

There was also more than a little irony attached to the outcome of the qualifying draw for the European Championships in the year 2000. The draw, made in Ghent on 18 January 1998, placed Scotland, once again, in the same section as Estonia. The Tartan Army were reassured that the game would be scheduled for daylight hours and that everything would be done to ensure that the Estonian team turned up. Next time around we will not need to look to Four Fingers to find the net.

CHAPTER 8

MONTE CARLO AND NEARLY BUST

THE BIZARRE EXPERIENCE AND OUTCOME of the 'ghost' game against Estonia in October '96 merely gave the Tartan Army new material to exploit for the rearranged game in Monaco. Concerned not to be denied their ninety minutes of football by deficient floodlighting for a second time, advance steps were set in motion. Craig 'Shaky' Steven gave himself the job of ensuring that members of the Edinburgh Tartan Army would have their own 'mobile' floodlights at the game.

Meanwhile, the task of finding budget accommodation on the Riviera was given to Johnny Marr. Being in the early stages of a new romance, maybe Johnny's mind was not on the 'correct' job. Working from a French holiday brochure giving details on accommodation on the Med, Johnny reached an advanced stage of booking digs for eight footsoldiers. He was very pleased with the deal he'd got for us. A very reasonable price for this part of the world. But a complication came to light when the intended host faxed back Johnny querying why the 'guests' had at least two names each and in some cases (John McIntosh Marr for instance) had three. The place he was on the verge of confirming turned out to be Monaco Kennel Club. Perhaps he should have just gone ahead with it. The Tartan Army have slept in a lot worse. Indeed, only a few weeks before the Baltic campaign, big Davie Lewis and Chiz, on their first night in Vienna for Scotland's first World Cup qualifying game against Austria, spent the night in a skip. They passed a relatively peaceful few hours, waking only when their accommodation began to move. The skip was being lifted.

Anyone fearing a repeat of the floodlighting problems experienced in Estonia could draw some confidence from the bags of tee-shirts which Davie Coutts had brought with him from Tallinn. These sported a picture of the Scotland manager's face with the words: 'And Craig said, 'let there be light, and there was light, and it was good' - Estonia versus Scotland, Louis II Stadium, Monaco, 11 February 1997.'

The portrait of Craig Brown on the tee-shirts, as far as its prediction about the lights was concerned, was accurate, but even

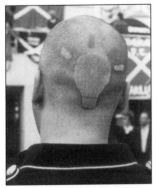

if it had not been the Edinburgh Tartan Army had come prepared. Shaky came through with 70 pairs of headlamps for distribution to the fans prior to the game. They were nifty wee yellow numbers, the kind that are shaped like a pair of specs with beams coming out of both legs. And Shaky himself was certainly taking no chances. He had his head completely shaved the night before he left Edinburgh. Shaved, that is, all but for

Shaky, a bit light-headed.

a tuft of hair at the back in the shape of a light bulb and which he dyed (or rather Anneli, his Finnish fiancee dyed) bright yellow.

But as for the game, the result (a 0:0 draw) turned out to be one of profound darkness for the large travelling support which had gathered behind the national team. In the intervening period since the Tallinn debacle, the likely turnout of fans at the game in Monaco had been a subject of considerable debate. 'Do you really think the fans will return for this one even if they are getting free tickets?' 'Naw, surely they will boycott it. Vote with their feet. People will

Where were you when the lights went out? Monaco.

just think they're mugs if they go?... ' This was the gist of much of what was being said at the time.

But it was already clear well before the date of the game that the Tartan Army was preparing to march in considerable number by the unusually high demand for tickets which Marjory Nimmo was handling. There were probably many reasons for this, some deeply psychological and none financial. But some were also pretty straightforward. Scotland had never played in Monte Carlo before and it seemed a pretty crazy place to stoat around in. Imagine it, the footsoldiers, a few unwashed and many unslept for days, rubbing shoulders with some of the world's richest, in one

Slumming it in Monte Carlo.

of the globe's glitziest places. And so it came to pass that the greatest travelling support the world has ever seen came to Monte Carlo.

Even a couple of days before the game the cafés and gardens outside Prince Rainier's casino, one of the landmarks of the Principality, were host to many fans relaxing and swallowing beer that was only fractionally cheaper than that served up in the Faroe Islands. 'Hey, this is a real cheap place' one of the troops was heard to say, not an uncommon remark among the fans when passing time in cripplingly expensive places. I recall Paddy McLaughlin saying something similar every time he bought a round in Sweden back in '92.

Many fans paid their 50 Francs to gain entry to the casino and were trying their luck at the gaming tables. And some were pretty lucky too, for a while. Johnny Marr had a fairly large lift, something in the region of a £1,000. But he too was soon down to his last chip, which was one chip more than his pal who was reduced to placing a solitary sugar lump on number 13.

Prior to the Monaco campaign, the fans had received a stern message about their behaviour and the need to avoid excessive drunkenness from the SFA. It has to be said that a number of the fans I spoke to were none to pleased about this, particularly when it was covered on the front page of the *Herald* the week before the game. For the benefit of people who are not in the SFA Travel Club, I should point out that every supporter who purchases a ticket from this source also receives a small Guidance Notes booklet giving helpful information about the place we are heading for. The booklet normally opens with a letter from the Manager to the fans. For many of us this is well appreciated. Its usual tone is that the person writing to the fans is a fan himself and would be on the terraces with the rest of us if it were not for his temporary tenure of what the great Jock Stein called 'an impossible job.' On this occasion the booklet opened with an unsigned message which many fans assumed could only have come from the SFA's Chief Executive, Mr Jim Farry. The bulk of the message is as follows:

> The reputation of Scotland and the sporting principles of our football supporters are again on trial. In recent matches foul language and offensive behaviour committed by a small number of 'supporters' have detracted from our excellent record. The Manager, his players and backroom staff, and all others connected with the S.F.A. work hard to provide every assistance for our supporters. Please respect their endeavours and display 'Fair Play' and proper respect for all others in Monaco: local residents, stadium authorities, police, our friends from Estonia (with whom we have no quarrel), the F.I.F.A. match officials; and, most importantly, the anthems of both countries and the pre-match ceremonies.

At the final whistle, and after what could be described as a disappointing but not surprising result when set in the context of Scotland's track record against minnows in important games abroad, 2,000 Tartan Army cheered and clapped the delighted

Estonians from the park. Some fans reserved a few jeers for our own players, most of whom looked crestfallen. One player was seen to mouth a few obscenities as fellow player Colin Calderwood acknowledged the fans and their disappointment.

The incident was caught on TV back home and, by the time the fans trooped back over the next few days, this had become big news. In fact, it became something of a scandal. Something, also, of a red face for the SFA in the light of the Association's stern letter to the fans. So, as the fans were showing 'Fair Play' and respect to our Estonian friends ('with whom we have no quarrel'), one of the players was busy swearing at the fans. Or was he? The player's agent was reported as saying that the player's anger was directed, not at the Scottish fans, but at the Estonian players. But we thought that these were people 'with whom we have no quarrel?' Whichever way you cut it the letter had created a hostage to fortune which rebounded on the author's pen.

Manager Craig Brown was left to face press and public questions in the immediate aftermath. 'If anything was said towards our fans I would take a very dim view of it in the light of what the fans mean to us,' was Craig's diplomatic and public position on the matter. Maybe some people who'd been at the game felt peeved about the incident, but I didn't meet any. The player's short profanity seems to have been a big deal to people back home, given the rush to voice an opinion which it generated. But as I recall Clint Eastwood remark with disdain in one of his movies, 'opinions are like arseholes, everybody's got one'. As far as I'm concerned, for the vast majority of the travelling support this was a non issue. The team manager had more important questions on his mind and I'm sure that he would have had a go at answering them had the small group of angry fans which confronted the team's coach as it left the stadium given him a chance.

The manager was diplomatic, as always, but by the following week the national press had rounded on the Tartan Army. One sports journalist, groping for the message he wished to convey wrote, '...let's face it these fans are..., well let's not beat about the bush, the Tartan Army are demented.' Another sports hack, who had previously accused the Tartan Army in the Faroes of doing more damage to Scotland than Margaret Thatcher, warned the SFA that it must not discipline the player because 'They cannot afford to allow the lunatics to take over the asylum.' He was supported by a former Lord Provost of Glasgow who declared that 'You wouldn't let these people into your garden let alone your living room.'

A former player, writing for an evening newspaper, lamented that the 'warmth and good humour for which the Scottish supporters were renowned appears to have evaporated,' citing the marvellous scenes in Seville back in '82 when the Tartan Army danced the samba with the victorious Brazilians as a thing of the distant past. But he seemed to forget that it had been the same in Turin during Italia '90, although the result that evening had been a much crueller pill to swallow than the '82 defeat by a Brazilian team not that far removed from greatness. And he couldn't have been in Birmingham in the Summer of '96 to see the Scots and Dutch fans marching arm and arm through the city centre, singing and waving to watching office staff, 'what's it like to be at work?'

The sound bite journalism which erupted in the wake of the Monaco incident brought to mind a more substantive piece which had appeared some months earlier in *Scotland on Sunday*. This was by Raymond Travers and was penned as another of his humourous '*IN THE DOCK*' articles. On this occasion, the 'Charge' was:

> Tartan Army, you have staggered into this courtroom, obstreperous with drink, to confront allegations that, while cavorting around the globe in an incoherent state of urine-sodden pandemonium while dressed like silly buggers, you sought to belittle the reputation of the diplomatic corps by posing as Cultural Ambassadors for your country.

In fact the whole piece merits reproduction in full (see next page). Quite outstanding. I'm for nominating Raymond Travers for the Nobel Prize in Journalism, if there is such an accolade. I was moved when I first opened my Sunday paper at this piece. It is rare, but so refreshing, to find an objective and quality piece of sports journalism these days.

In the Dock No 4... **Tartan Army**

THE CHARGE

Tartan Army, you have staggered into this courtroom, obstreperous with the drink, to confront allegations that, while cavorting around the globe in an incoherent state of urine-sodden pandemonium while dressed like silly buggers, you sought to belittle the reputation of the diplomatic corps by posing as Cultural Ambassadors for your country.

THE PROSECUTION

From Moscow to Mendoza, this rabblous gaggle have marauded in search of cheap swally and casual fornication. Fountains have been polluted, flowerbeds soiled and public conveniences body-swerved as these enuretic hordes cut a steaming swathe through town. But who, exactly, are they, these pishing pirates of Brown Army, and what do they want? A recent undercover investigation by the SFA's top brassiere dispelled persistent rumours that the Scotland Travel Club had been infiltrated by a breakaway faction of Germany's notorious Bladder-Meinhoff Gang. Others have claimed that miserable and monotonous hen-pecked domestic existences have been responsible for grown men donning "Scots On The Bevvy" tee-shirts and acting like bewhiskied bozos the moment international territory has been reached.

But, members of the jury, I ask you this: when was the last time you witnessed a bona fide cultural ambassador ask of a foreign lady, "Want a stroke o'ma sporran, darlin'?" Or lurch miroculously down the Champs-Elysees with bottles of cheap table wine clinking sonorously in that suitcase of the dispossessed, a poly bag?

Complaints have emanated from many sources throughout football's sprawling diaspora. The Noise Abatement Society, in particular, have habitually had their frayed tethers distended with raucous renditions of the Jimmy Hill song, a chant some claim is a disgusting slander on the good name of poofs everywhere. For those present in this courtroom who may be unfamiliar with Mr Hill, let me affirm that he is a respected and knowledgeable figure adored by generations of football connoisseurs.

At this juncture I would like to express a few words of praise about the admirable contribution of the SFA regarding this grave matter. Mr Farry and his able band of flunkies have tried doggedly to stamp out the uncouth and anti-social deportment of these rogue elements within the international team's support. All members of the Scotland Travel Club have been issued with elegant crest-embazoned ties or spiffing blue and white scarves in an attempt to alienate the slovenly contingent. But still the urinating continues.

I believe it was Kevin Drinkell who once mused, "I would rather have a bottle in front of me than a frontal lobotomy". I assert that the Tartan Army have already acquired both and it is for this reason that I urge the full weight of the jury's outrage be reflected in an appropriate sentence.

CASE FOR THE DEFENCE

Your assertion that a politically disenfranchised Scotland requires as much visibility as it can possible muster on foreign soil, is categorically no excuse of the inebriated Nationalistic outpourings you so overpoweringly exhibit.

VERDICT

Guilty as charged. For the duration of every ensuing Scottish International, you shall be transported to joyless dreary outposts such as Iran, Saudi Arabia and Dundee, whereby any public displays of passing your water shall result in immediate genital surgery. Take them down.

Raymond Travers

We may not have lived up to Mr Travers' high expectations, but certainly no one could have confused the Tartan Army, for the few days we were cavorting around the south of France, with church mice. Our group was based in Nice and had a ball of a

time bouncing between bars and one Karaoke club in particular. We billeted ourselves in the small Hotel Gounod, a charming wee place with incredibly tolerant staff and appropriately located in a street called 'Rue Meyerbeer.'

Street of Dreams: the local 'offie' on the Rue Meyerbeer.

Johnny Marr had come good in the end. There was not a kennel in sight. However, a few days later on the promenade in Monte Carlo we chanced upon 'The Monaco Kennel Club.' 'So is this where you were going to have us staying Johnny? Lets check it out,' declared Psycho Sid. The bell was duly rung. On opening the door, a charming looking lady could not have been more helpful when met with the request 'Can we see the dogs please?' The beasts certainly had it pretty good. We would have been comfortable there, but Johnny's choice of the Hotel Gounod just shaded it.

However, the night before he left Edinburgh for Nice, Johnny was truer to form. A few weeks earlier he had decided that it would be a nice touch to organise a surprise golden anniversary for his mother. The word was spread among the relatives. Aunts, uncles and cousins from down south and up north descended on the Portobello boarding house Johnny had arranged for the occasion. The cake was there and everything was set. The day before the big event Johnny was so excited he just couldn't keep it a secret any longer and proudly broke the news to his mum. The dutiful son. Dutiful maybe, but with a poor memory for dates. Her golden anniversary was not for another year.

Johnny was glad to get away to Nice which was having a carnival at the time. Perfect cover for the troops. As part of the carnival, huge papier mâché figures had been made up and placed around the town. Some of these were recruited and, over the next few days, could be seen weaving their way through the streets of Nice in the company of kilted footsoldiers.

'Anyone fancy a relaunch of the Tartan Navy - The Faroes, once more wi' feelin'?' was suggested, provoking a discussion about how we should get to the game.

'Naw, it'll no be the same,' said Johnny sadly, 'Mad Dog and Gudge are no here. And that means we'll have no puffins. You need puffins to be the Tartan Navy.'

'Well how about if we get one of these big radge papier mâché guys to sail the boat,' suggested Martin Riddell. 'Won't that look mental when we sail up next to these big fuck off yachts in Monte Carlo with a 14 foot monster at the helm?'

'Ah did'ne know Colin MacDonald was a sailor,' murmured Safe Hands.

'Watch it you,' warned big Colin for whom the campaign had been touch and go till the last minute due to a severe bout of gout.

The boat idea caught on fast and by Monday morning enquiries were in motion. Marr was getting excited again. 'Yeh, lets buy plastic swords and eye patches. We can kid on we're pirates, board the fanciest yacht, drink their best wine then kidnap the owner's wife and take her to the game.'

The planning had started too soon and it turned out that no boat got hired. But the usual minor travel cock ups and other incidents transpired. Four Fingers, who arrived on the Monday and found when trying to check into the Quality Hotel that someone calling themselves Tam Ritchie had cancelled his room, caught a train to Cannes instead of Monte Carlo. Johnny and me got a lift back in the boot of a car with the Canadian ski team and then taught them how to go 'downhill' in Nice.

Danny Divers, who'd no intention of going to the game, but who had opened his pub in Dunstable for us between Easy Jet flights in Luton, ended up on the end of a whip round and was flown out on the last empty seat on the day of the game. Danny's last remaining seat on the return flight the next morning remained empty. Tam had 'rescued' him from a night on the beach promising Danny he'd get him to the airport on time. Another of Tam's plans! Danny had fallen for the curse of Four Fingers. He eventually escaped from the twisted clutches of the deformed one and was befriended by a carload of footsoldiers on their way back to the Globe Bar in Dumfries.

Hell mend Danny. He should have known better. Disaster is a fate which beckons anyone daft enough to throw in their lot with Four Fingers. Tam's wee English mate Mark Anderson, another taxi driver from Stockport, will testify to that. Despite having travelled with Tam to see Scotland in Sweden in May '97, he travelled again to the friendly against France in St Etienne the following November. Mark found himself alone, lost and knackered early in the morning. Fortune had it that he stumbled upon Grigor's coach. He tried the luggage compartment . It was open. Magic. So in he goes to get the head down for a couple of hours and pulls the door shut behind him. Waking up bursting for a pee he discovered that the compartment was not intended for accommodation. The door could not be opened from the inside. After enduring a lengthy period of pain, rolling over and pressing his wee man against the side of the bus, he did his best to direct the jet of urine towards a hairbreadth of light at the bottom of the door. This proved less than successful. He lay in the darkness, relieved, but very damp, for several hours until his banging and shouting attracted the attention of an early morning street cleaner.

Excessive celebration leads to casualties and there were a few of these in and around Nice. However, I for one never expected that I'd hear as strange a tale as Jimmy Cormack told me about when he was in Nice during Italia '90. Then, the night's action was beginning to wind down. Pubs in Nice's main street closed at 2am and Jimmy Cormack and a pal from Partick were quietly finishing off their last litre of beer that evening. The noisiest man in the street joined them. Former Scotland stalwart Kenny Burns, one of the hardest defenders of the '70s and a fine servant to the national cause, was not for calling it a night quite yet.

'C'mon boys we're goin' for a swim' Kenny insisted. As Jimmy and his mate followed him across the Boulevard Maritime, Kenny leapt up onto the parapet which ran along the esplanade. A momentary pause to glance back and check the boys were in tow, then a head first dive into the blackness towards the sea. But the sea was not there. Worse still. What was mostly a pebble beach was at that point a collection of very large boulders which Kenny met head on. Jimmy was mightily impressed, 'Kenny Burns? That's one hard guy,' he has said on many an occasion since.

Dazed and very bloody, Kenny groaned himself to his feet, groped along the sea wall till he found a set of steps, and hauled his way back up onto the esplanade. Jimmy could see at a glance that Kenny was seriously in need of medical attention and fortunately managed to flag down a passing ambulance. Jimmy bundled him into the vehicle then climbed in himself, sufficiently concerned to accompany the injured one to hospital. On arrival, the unfortunate Burns was immediately whisked away for treatment.

Peering over the Esplanade in Monaco, just in case some other idiot has taken a header onto the beach.

Meanwhile, Jimmy, blood-soaked and knackered, remained alone in the waiting room, intending to hang back and see what was happening. The heat and the drink soon took effect and Jimmy nodded off. He recalls coming round with a start, lying flat out on an operating table, staring up at bright lights with a doctor and two nurses poking him to try and find where all the blood was coming from. They must have got a hellava shock when Jimmy sprang to his feet, screamed 'there's nothin' wrang wi me' and made off along the corridor doing a fair impression of Alan Wells. This was before the World Cup had started, but Jimmy never set eyes on Kenny Burns again.

It was probably the Hospital St Roch that Kenny and Jimmy

were in. It was certainly the St Roch that Johnny and Andy of the Edinburgh Tartan Army were in during the wee small hours of the Monday morning. Andy had taken a bad turn which he later attributed to something he ate (which must have been three days before) and a kindly bar manager had called an ambulance. Only one of the troops was allowed to travel with him. On arrival Andy was wheeled away and Johnny, as did Jimmy Cormack almost 7 years earlier, fell asleep. It was the slight discomfort in the left hand which woke him. He opened his eyes to see a trickle of blood and a doctor inserting a needle into his vein. A little explanation and as sober a posture as he could manage and Johnny was soon on his way out of there, resolving to return and check on his friend later in the morning.

Andy woke a couple of hours later, to no little surprise, to find himself in an empty room with a drip attached to the back of his left hand. After checking both arms and legs were moving and feeling around the rest of his body with his free hand, he declared himself fit for another day of manoeuvres, disconnected the drip needle and started looking for his pair of ghillie brogues. These he found in an annex room and he was soon out in the fresh morning air without having seen another soul in the hospital. On arriving back at the Hotel Gounod, he woke Johnny who was his room mate and the troops were soon regrouping in the foyer.

Other casualties were rather more severe. The 'Half Wick' from Wick, who had travelled with us in the minivan taxi four months earlier between Riga and Tallinn, received a nasty slash on the stomach courtesy of an Algerian thug. An Aberdonian, surprisingly this was not 'Lucky' Murray, ended up in hospital after being stabbed in the back when he and his pal were returning home late at night. A husband and wife who were on holiday in the Bordeaux region of France, and who had travelled to Nice to take in the game, got caught up in festivities to the wife's detriment. She had slipped and broke her hip when dancing. 'Nae luck,' mourned Safe Hands, 'I guess you just never know the minute.' 'Yeah, I suppose so,' agreed the husband, 'but the wet coffee table she was dancing on certainly didnae help.' 'So what are you going to do now?' big Colin enquired. 'Well, they say she has to stay in hospital for about two weeks.' 'So are you looking for a hotel to hang on here?' 'No way, I'm going back to Bordeaux. It's great there.'

Hence, it came to pass that the boot swung in the Baltics was followed through in Monaco leaving Bonnie Scotland, in the words of manager Craig Brown, with 'a mountain to climb' in the quest to reach the World Cup Finals in France. The Tartan Army looked again to Julie Andrews for inspiration. There is more than one song that can be lifted from the *Sound of Music*. By the close of play on the 11 February 1997, *Doe a Deer's* grip at the top of the Tartan Army charts was looking vulnerable to another of the bold Julie's numbers: *Climb Every Mountain*.

'That was definitely my last trip,' announced Marr, wearing a bugs bunny waist pouch around his neck, as we waited to change planes back at Luton airport. Another Edinburgh Tartan Army member nodded vigorously in agreement, a child's mini mouse rucksack strapped to the back of his piper's jacket and the mouse's head also nodding in the affirmative. Another couple of ales were downed and we began our farewells. Most of the boys were flying to Edinburgh and Auld Davie, Willie Scott and me were heading for Glasgow. 'Well, Johnny, if I happen to miss you in Kilmarnock or at Parkhead, shall I see you in Gothenburg in April?' I asked. 'Definitely, I've got a good feeling about that one,' Marr waved back.

Around the same time that we were bidding each other farewell, another two members of the Edinburgh Tartan Army, Jim Briggs and Paul 'Pud' Smith, were just about to leave a fancy restaurant in Monte Carlo and head to the Nice Airport. They had just completed a sombre 'next day' post-mortem of what had gone wrong at the game the night before. Jim was

Overcome with emotion, Big Davie faints.

Estonia in Monaco. No matter how bad things get, always remember, it has been a lot worse.

mourning not having stuck to their original plan. Earlier the previous day they had discovered that the Estonian team were also staying in the Hotel Abela. On checking in they spotted the players standing in the foyer. The players saw them too. 'You could see their hearts visibly sink when they saw us,' said Jim. Naturally, Pud and Jim resolved to return to the hotel that evening at a reasonable hour and commence an all night ceilidh. But by the time they got back, breakfast was being served and the opportunity to deny Scotland's opponents their forty winks was gone.

Before they reached the door of the restaurant the manageress came over to say that one of the Scotland players was eating in the restaurant. They guessed it must be John Collins who played his club football for Monaco. Pud asked the lady if she would mind asking John if they could say hello and minutes later they joined the player and his parents for a chat at their table. 'Aw, you pair laddies. A' this way tae see Johnny and the team play like that,' was his mum's first words. They spent some time swapping stories when Jim was forced to interrupt one of John's tales. 'John, listen, it's been great to meet you and we'd like to talk longer. But we've got to go. Out helicopter is waiting.' His folks smiled and John just laughed. 'Nice people,' said Pud as they flew the short 10 minute stretch to the airport.

CHAPTER 9

THERE'S NO SUCH THING AS AN UGLY SWEDE

YOU COULD SEE AULD DAVIE AND WILLIE SCOTT in the Ullevi Stadium in Gothenburg. They were just down below where I was standing with Fat Graham and Gavin, two final year university students, as we waved large plastic SNP placards. Auld Davie and Willie were just along a bit from crazy Jimmy Simons from Dunfermline. My mind started to stray to over five years back when Crazy Jimmy stopped the train on the way back from Norrköping to Gothenburg, but the memory of Crazy Jimmy took a back seat when I caught sight of the auld yins in their kilts. So they were as good as their word when they had promised a few weeks before to wear the full regalia for the Sweden game in April 1997.

'I've no had the kilt on for 47 years' Auld Davie had protested that Saturday morning in Heilan Jessie's pub next to Glasgow's Barras. That had been back in Palestine where Auld Davie had been on guard duty at the King David Hotel, or rather had just finished duty, handing over to the Americans, when a terrorist milk truck rolled in and blew the place to bits. I had heard that story before, but that morning in Heilan Jessie's was the first time I'd heard the auld yin chuckle as he recalled holding up a brothel in the Heliopolis district in Cairo, again in full regalia. 'We were called the 'swingin sixes' because of the six tassels in the Argyle's sporran,' Davie explained. 'And were you just yourself?,' I asked. 'Oh no, I was in the company of Nobbie Clark and Rab McKay, and a Lee Enfield 303.'

Although soldiering in Cairo was thirsty work, they had only managed to swally part of their spoils before they were standing in line with other squaddies from the Argyle and Sutherland Highlanders making up an identity parade. The madam must have taken a shine to them, or she possibly felt they were merely borrowing back what had been their own cash, because she did not pick them out. It's a wee bit hard to believe, but Auld Davie claims she gave him a wink on the way past. Well, after 47 years, time and tide waits for no man, but Auld Davie, and Willie too, looked outstanding in full regalia.

A couple of nights later, now back in Copenhagen, a bloke from Cumbernauld got the surprise of his life. Willie, Auld Davie, Gordon 'Safe' Hands and big Colin MacDonald were having a few late beers in the Spunk Bar just round the corner from the Hotel Centrum where we were staying. Willie had retired to the Hotel just before the guy from Cumbernauld arrived. 'You've just missed Chick Murray, you know,' said the auld yin. 'Chick Murray? I thought he was deid. Is he no deid?' The bloke from Cumbernauld was confused and not too sure of his ground. 'He's no the man he used to be, but he made it here all the same' said Auld Davie. 'In fact if you'd like to meet him we might just catch him before he goes to his bed.'

'Safe' Hands could see what was going down and slipped away to alert Willie who was having a night-cap in the hotel foyer. Five minutes at his back and in rolls Auld Davie with the Cumbernauld guy in tow. 'There ye go son, meet Chick Murray.' The bloke was really wasted. 'My dad is a great fan of yours Mr Murray, I only wish he was here to meet you himself. Would it be OK if we got a photograph together?' Chick duly obliged. ' Oh this is great. I got my photo taken with Jim Leighton in Gothenburg two days ago. Photos with two famous people in the one week. I canny believe it.'

One week before, we had met up with Gus Clark and big Davie Lewis in the Spunk bar. They had come out on the early morning flight with 'Shaky' Steven and Anneli. They looked not bad and had held themselves together pretty well for a day on the drink. They had had a brief respite from the beer when unexpectedly confronted by a Swedish TV crew at the airport.

Swedish TV interview Scottish Ambassador. (Didn't ask for the name of his hairdresser.)

Shaky handled the interview while Gus and big Davie did the Hokey Cokey, accompanied with the following lyrics:

You put your left leg in,
Your left leg out,
Your left leg in and you shake it all about,
You do the Tommy Brolin and you turn around,
That's what it's all about.
Oh Tommy, Tommy Brolin,
Oh Tommy, Tommy Brolin,
Oh Tommy, Tommy Brolin,
He put the English OUT OUT OUT

This jig which has become a firm favourite with the Tartan Army since 1992 when Brolin's goal in Stockholm sent England crashing out of Euro '92. I remember watching the game in a pub in Gothenburg. The next morning about 60 of the troops were marching along the Avenue holding up the back page of a national daily with Brolin's picture singing 'One Tommy Brolin, there's only one Tommy Brolin...' It was yet another one of a number of important bonding moments with the Swedes.

Similar happenings were also taking place in the small Swedish town of Jönköping, where the Partick Thistle International Supporters Section decided to base themselves during Euro '92. I'll let Tommy Madden tell you about it for himself:

Jim Brown and myself made contact with the Town Hall to announce our arrival and to arrange a date to see the Mayor. Contact made, the town became our adopted city and the TV cameras were our constant companions. The Town Hall made sure that we were never short of a lift on a police motorbike or had to wait in queues for night clubs. We were the Scots, and we were good. The Hotel Klosterkungen made sure that Swedish ladies were welcome, but Swedish laddies were by invitation only. Summoned to the Town Hall, Jim and myself set off bearing gifts and good tidings from the City of Glasgow. The reception was formal with wine and canapes. We returned the invitation for the Mayor to join us back at the Klosterkungen to watch the Sweden v England game. We assured the Mayor that Paul 'Pud' Smith had sufficient Glenmorangie to keep him happy. What a night! Sweden and Tommy Brolin murdered England. The poor Mayor was so overcome by emotion and Glenmorangie that we had to carry him out to his limousine.

'Sure, I'll come back for a drink with you.'
Famous last words from the Mayor of Jönköping.

But let's get back to the Swedish trip in April 1997. A new friend joined us during our first few days in Copenhagen. Naomi was her name. We met her in a shop in the red light area just around the corner from the Spunk Bar. 'What colour would you like?' asked the shopkeeper. 'What colours have you got?' replied the Edinburgh Tartan Army footsoldier. The colour choice was not varied. There was black and there was white, and they all had big red lips and wore a wide mouth expression that one of the more cultured among the Tartan Army pointed out looked like the face in Edvard Munch's famous painting *The Scream.*

'The Tartan Army are not racist,' declared one of the troops as the other heads nodded. So out we went with Naomi. She was quickly inflated, equipped with tartan scarf and topped off with a Balmoral. Naomi's ego must have been well chuffed as she became the centre of attention for tourists with their cameras as she sat proudly in her supermarket trolley outside the Dubliner pub, giving the chaos inside a rest for a while. Once or twice the attention drifted away from Naomi.

On one occasion we were joined by a couple of street musicians, a husband and wife pairing it seemed. The guy, who looked like a Danish version of Ian Munro, worked the squeeze box while his wife played exquisitely on a saw with a violin rod.

We lost Naomi in Copenhagen. Anyway she was past her best and had started to deflate during the afternoon. All the rough treatment she'd received (dancing; swinging from lights; drinking on an empty stomach) had taken its toll. Her failing health drew the attention of a concerned Jimmy Cormack whose roll of SNP stickers served as emergency first aid for Naomi. A few strategically positioned stickers gave Naomi a new leaf of life. In fact Jimmy's stickers seemed to get everywhere. Young children in particular were a favourite target. Hundreds of kids were walking around Copenhagen, Gothenburg and the other Swedish town of Helsingborg sporting an aspiration for Scottish independence a few days before Britain's epoch making General Election of May 1997.

Maybe had Scotland taken something from the game against Sweden on the Wednesday night a stronger Nationalist vote might have been delivered back home the next day. But it was not for want of trying by the fans in the stadium in Gothenburg. On the day of the game, Jim Briggs took delivery of a box of the one meter long plastic 'Vote SNP - Best for Scotland' placards

'C'mon gie's a shot of your beard.'
The street musician refuses to entertain Auld Davie's request.

which had been brought over by two party workers. These certainly attracted some airtime as they were waved enthusiastically during the match by members of the Tartan Army.

Proof that Shaky does not go about with his head up his own arse all of the time.

Only one of the troops involved seemed less than happy to play his part in the political campaign. That was Psycho Sid. A close inspection of Sid's placard revealed the following words, written in biro: 'Psycho Sid Says Vote Tory.'

However, the game and the General Election were still ahead of us as we left Copenhagen for Sweden, travelling on a cloud of expectation. We said farewell to our friends in the Dubliner on the Sunday and crossed to the port of Helsingborg. We knew we'd see the Dubliner lads again as they were running a bus up to Gothenburg for the game. But we didn't expect to be back in a Dubliner so quick. Good God, these pubs are all over the place! There was another one right across the road from Helsingborg railway station.

It was Sunday, mid-afternoon, and the fifteen of us in transit had half an hour or so to kill before the 4 hour train ride from to Gothenburg. 'Anyone fancy a quick pint,' asked Psycho Sid, turning round to speak to the rest of our group which was already half way across the road. The quick pint took just short of a full day and we managed to board a train to Gothenburg around lunchtime on the Monday. Once again the hospitality was immense. Eamonn Fagen, the manager, who spent most of the time in a green piper's jacket, and Kim the cook, did the boys proud. 'We'll sort out a bed for the old guys and the rest of you can just camp out in the pub,' said Eamonn. Tam Scones took him literally. He opened up his rucksack, pitched his tent next to the bar, using the footrest as support for the guy rope, and crawled into his sleeping bag.

Yes, tents can come in handy even when you don't need them and have been a common item in many footsoldiers' luggage over the years. Frank The Wank from Clydebank, who we met early on in the book, had his tent with him in Tel Aviv in 1981 when Kenny's goal gave us a 0:1 victory over Israel in the qualifying for the '82 World Cup in Spain. FTW, as he is known, possibly forgot he was travelling in style and had a room to himself in one of the plushest hotels in the city. But Frank had gone prepared for the possibility of an accommodation shortage. Not wishing to be accused of carrying useless items Frank pitched the tent in his hotel bedroom. It was perfectly erected. Well almost. Frank's only mistake was to attach one of the main guy ropes to a moveable item: the inside handle of the room door. Jimmy Thorburn (the guy Jim Manual found comatose in a bush in Acapulco) popped up to raise Frank a couple of times and on each occasion Frank awoke with the tent falling about his ears.

Back in '92 Wee Geordie recalls arriving in Gothenburg by ferry in the company of a guy from Glasgow who was even more skint than he was and who was managing to get by, not on a

Leslie's first campaign. The Tartan Army get an election.

shoestring, but on a tent. Despite his financial embarrassment the wee fella had saved hard to buy his match tickets and stretched his budget to a seat on a bus. His total financial resources to sustain him through the Swedish campaign was his giro.

The guy's first problem was getting into Sweden. At the ferry terminal's passport control his bedraggled appearance attracted the attention of a vigilant policeman. The lack of gear, apart from a small scabby tent bag, caused particular concern. 'But you cannot come in to the country without clothes,' announced the policeman. Things looked bleak for the wee guy until a voice from behind announced 'Here's his stuff here, I'm carrying it for him,' and a rucksack was promptly emptied onto the ground. The policeman reached forward and held up a pair of jeans. They came up to the wee guy's chin. He just laughed, shook his head and waved them all through.

When the coach arrived at the campsite in Norrköping the tent bag was tossed into the field and he set off to see how far the giro would go. Not far at Swedish prices but enough for one good session. Later on, and too pished to erect the tent, he settled down in the open air for the night. In the early hours he was woken by a Swedish lady passing on her bike. She was either a nurse or a midwife coming home from a night shift. She was extremely concerned about the wee fella's homeless state. 'A'm aw right dear. A'm gist tryin tae get some kip. Nae problem. A've a tent in the field ower therr. A'll get it later.' But the Swedish Florence Nightingale persisted. His protests were brushed aside. He was bundled up and drooped over the handlebars as she set off into the field in search of his unpacked accommodation. This girl could not be stopped. With the wee yin still protesting he was OK she put up his tent and didn't leave until she saw him safely inside. Later that morning he surfaced to find a bag of messages at the front of the tent. And this was not the last he heard from her. Although he never set eyes on her again, the kindly Swedish tooth fairy returned several times, depositing a food parcel on each visit.

Having all but sorted out his food situation the wee fella was left with the problem of how to buy his bevy. As the good book says, man cannot live by bread alone. Well, with the best part of two weeks to go this is where the tent came in real handy. A market opportunity was spotted. The tents of the Tartan Army were congested and some of the lads found this greatly inconvenient when bringing female guests back to the camp site. A spare tent, where they could be alone to recite the poems of Rabbie Burns without disturbing the rest of their pals, was just what was needed. This line of trade generated sufficient revenue to buy around ten beers a day, which is no mean feat at Swedish prices.

The Tartan Army have always spent generously in Sweden. Ian, the bloke who had opened the Dubliner in Gothenburg just before Euro '92, insists that Scotland's visit for the Championships was what made him. Ian went out of his way to make the troops welcome in his bar on the Avenue when we returned in '97. Fat Graham had been wandering up the Avenue at 6am in the morning. He was wondering what had become of his pal Gavin, although he had a pretty good idea. 'Is that a noise I hear?' said Graham to himself as he was passing the Dubliner. 'No that's not a 'noise'. That's a commotion and it can only mean one thing.' Inside, amongst others, he found Alan Jamieson from Shetland and a piper. As the merriment continued, Ian, the manager, announced that he had to go home to meet his girlfriend. As the piper played *Danny Boy,* Ian left the keys of the pub with Alan. 'Would you mind taking care of the pub for a couple of hours. The cleaners are due in about 9am.' And rather startled cleaners they were too. The sight which met them was more like 9 at night than 9 in the morning. A smaller band of Tartan Army, but the party was still in full swing. Alan was using the tube off of the cleaner's hoover as a makeshift didgeridoo to accompany the piper.

Fat Graham and Gavin were on manoeuvres for the first time. However, the trip did not come at a good time in their youthful careers. 'I can't believe they're doing this,' said one of their fellow students back at the University, 'the finals start a week after they get back.' Yes, while Graham and Gavin were losing their Tartan Army virginity on the Swedish campaign, their classmates were losing sleep revising well into the wee hours for exams that would decide what class of degree they would be walking away with after 4 years in higher education. Graham and Gavin might not have realised it at the time, but the piper has to be paid. And paid he was. When the degree results were announced a couple of months later they emerged at the bottom of their class.

It was good to see so many first timers with the Tartan Army in Sweden. It was the first campaign for Leslie Ingles (who added a bit of glamour to the proceedings), Pat Kelly and Craig Darling. All were new members of the Edinburgh Tartan Army. They made a fine contribution to our merry band and Pat and Craig were responsible for adding the 'tactical scratch' to the Tartan Army's repertoire. The appropriate time to apply the 'scratch' is when you are walking in front of a group of girls whose attention is on the swing of the kilts. The technique is a straightforward one.

You reach behind with one hand, left or right it doesn't matter, casually slide up the pleats of the kilt and scratch the itchy part of the buttock. The scratch's real value lies in its educational function in helping reduce the number of people who may later confront a footsoldier with that banal question, 'Is it true that a Scotsman...'

Leslie with Scott Paterson of the Canadian Tartan Army outside the Ullevi Stadium, Gothenburg.

But novices learn too. Craig Darling, who had come through to Glasgow for the flight out because he was on a 'two for one' ticket, was nobody's darlin' on the way home. The Copenhagen-Glasgow flight made its scheduled stop to drop off passengers at Edinburgh and Craig, booked through to Glasgow, decided that the simplest thing was to leave with Marr, Safe Hands, big Colin MacDonald and Swift. His bags were still in the hold and were going where he should have been. But this was not an issue for

Craig who was just looking forward to his bed. The Edinburgh boys had cleared the terminal and were well on their way while the Glasgow contingent and a large group of middle aged Danes heading for a golfing holiday were still sitting on the tarmac. The stewardess was 'sorry for the delay' but they had 'lost a passenger whose baggage is in the hold' and it was impossible to leave until the mystery was solved. The outcome? Everyone had to disembark and identify their luggage which by this time was spread out on the tarmac. Once the rogue bag belonging to the virgin had been identified and removed we were free to leave: a delay of only an hour and a half.

The virgins also made an impact on the plane out. We got talking to a couple of South African women who were, surprisingly, interested in the kilt. 'You know, we thought Scots were kidding when they said they wear nothing under their kilts. But when we were in the centre of Edinburgh earlier today a car dropped off a couple of people in Princes Street and the driver sounded the horn as he drove away. The two guys turned around, bent over, lifted their kilts and showed their bare bum to the car. We couldn't believe it.' At this point Craig and Pat turned around, named the time and place that the event took place and accurately described the car. Small world.

A few of the lads used the return to Sweden as a chance to celebrate happy occasions. Mikey Knep from Aberdeen, due to tie the knot with wee Fiona the following week, organised his stag on the Monday night. Another group, which included Billy Wilson from Pittenweem, could be distinguished by their 'Catherine's Army' teeshirts: a baby's head with tartan tammy. They were spending the best part of a week wetting the baby's head. They did a right good job of it too, so much so that after the match against Sweden, Billy Wilson turned to Marr and sighed 'well lets face it, it was great goal the Austrians scored.'

That comment put me in mind of Ian Mackie, another Vale Bar regular, at the Yugoslavia game in Belgrade several years before. Ian had travelled out on his todd without a ticket. He was feeling pretty pleased with himself having acquired a brief outside the ground for a fraction of the price fans paid back in Scotland.

Ian recalls being really surprised at the way the game was going, and even although he was among the home supporters he was getting no hassle whatever. The boys in blue were well on top but went a goal behind. But there was something else not right. He had heard about the internal tensions within Yugoslavia. Was this why the fans were not getting behind their team? And they seemed to like Scotland. Why? Ian eventually had it sussed when the boys in blue scored. The home fans erupted. Scotland were playing in white and Ian had been shouting for Yugoslavia.

A school teacher friend of mine was just a few yards away from me in the Ullevi Stadium, but I wasn't to know. He had self-certified himself sick from school and had acquired long black hair. The hair (a wig) along with a pair of dark sunglasses, gave him the security of knowing that even if the TV camera caught him in the crowd, colleagues watching back home would be unlikely to recognise him. The plan worked to perfection. He'd got the idea of 'disguise on manoeuvres' from Jimmy Manual a few years earlier.

Manual may have been posted missing in Gothenburg, but *Blue Peter* was there, represented by John Leslie, popular presenter of the long running children's TV programme. There he was, in the midst of the surrounding bedlam in the Dubliner, attracting attention from fans and critics alike. John was looking decidedly edgy when the fans enquired about his degree of intimacy with socialite and star of *The Darling Buds of May*, Catherine Zeta Jones. John was playing down any suggestion of a romantic link. But his case floundered when the troops burst into a rendition of 'Stand up if you've shagged Catherine Zeta Jones, stand up if you've...,' then sat down at the same time, leaving John as the only one standing. John took it all in good humour.

Another visitor to the Dubliner was a certain Henry Hodge, Vice Consul from the British Embassy in Stockholm. Henry and a colleague were in Gothenburg in an official capacity, to observe the behaviour of this particular group of fans from Britain. Danny Divers and myself came across Henry in the bar at the Sheraton Hotel after the match.

'So you were at the game then,' said Danny. 'Can you prove it?'

'What do you mean? replied Henry looking rather lost.

'Well, if you were there you'd be able to tell us what the fans sang for 20 minutes after the game. If fact, let's hear you sing it.' And sing it he did. There was the bold Henry, from the diplomatic corps, giving *Doe a Deer* laldy in the middle of the Sheraton.

We took Henry and his pal up to the Dubliner to join the party. Henry took note of the special affection which exists between the Swedes and the Scots. He could see the delight on the faces of the Swedes as the Tartan Army sang 'There's no such f★★★★★★ thing as an ugly Swede, there's no such f★★★★★★ thing as an ugly Swede...' to the tune of 'Ye canny push yer granny aff a bus.' The Swedes, who can speak better English than most of the Tartan Army, loved it. As Henry eventually called it a night he shook Danny's hand and thanked him 'for one of the most enjoyable nights of my life.'

Maybe Henry will reappear at another Scotland away game. If he does, he certainly won't be the first Englishman in the Tartan Army. Four Fingers had his wee pal Mark from Stockport with him. 'As English as the Pennine Hills,' as Four Fingers says. They had come with Grigor's mob, by boat from Harwich to Gothenburg. 'It was weird,' Tam recalled, 'when we boarded there was not a kilt in sight. Everyone was in plain clothes. I thought for a minute that I was on the wrong boat. Then about ten minutes into the sail the full regalia was out and everything was back to normal.' A lot of the boys got caught up in the gambling, betting £40 at a time on wooden horses and the roll of a dice. 'And did you try your luck?' I asked, knowing full well that bookies could quite safely tear up the betting slips before they give them to Tam. 'No way. I've got enough trouble betting on real horses let alone wooden ones.' Others in Grigor's party swerved the gambling and got themselves involved with a team of Swedish girls: the Swedish under 18 rugby team which was on its way home from a tournament.

The Tartan Navy made the crossing on the Monday night which meant Tam and Mark announced their arrival at our pension early on the Tuesday morning. After the briefest of visits they were persuaded to leave and set off for their own digs to try and catch some breakfast. The ladies were just cleaning up when Tam and his pal arrived in the breakfast room. 'They were really helpful. We asked for some toast and tea and they told us to sit down and they went away to get it for us.' Once fed and watered they went up to the room, but the key wouldn't work. 'There is something wrong with this key,' Tam explained to the lady at reception, 'it does not work in the door.' The lady inspected the key, tactfully trying to keep her eyes from Tam's deformed paw. 'There is nothing wrong with this key sir. You are in the wrong hotel.'

A few days earlier when we were still in Copenhagen, Willie Scott thought he was in the wrong country. 'Isn't that great' he had said as we had our first beer at Glasgow Airport. 'I told my neighbour about our trip and he bought me a guidebook.' 'Aye nice touch,' one of us remarked, knowing fine well that the Tartan Army cannot be confused with 'culture vultures'. The guide book reappeared when we arrived in the centre of Copenhagen and started to look for the Hotel Centrum. 'Look here, this book will tell us all we need to know,' declared Willie. 'Aye, maybe if we were looking for a hotel in Holland,' big Colin pointed out, having just noticed that Willie's neighbour had presented him with a guidebook for Amsterdam. Willie palmed it off with some comment about his neighbour not being the full shilling, prone to getting a bit confused and not taking in what Willie had told him about his travel itinerary. But Willie found it more difficult to deflect the troops' abuse when he was caught trying to pay for his first round of beers in Dutch Guilders.

The Swedish town of Trollhättan hosted the under 21 game the day before the big team took on Sweden in the World Cup game. A few hundred troops made the journey on a drizzly afternoon and found that the small town was having a Scottish week. As our group got off the train we walked straight into a pipe band being followed with what must have been a substantial proportion of the town's school population. After the game the railway station was heaving with tartan as folk waited over an hour for train back to Gothenburg. Everyone made it onto the train. Rather surprising as it is common to see a few forlorn faces still on the platform as trains pull away.

Trollhättan is only around three-quarter of an hour train ride from Gothenburg. The return train journey passed without incident, which gave me time to reflect on the last train ride back to Gothenburg I'd been on. That was back in '92 after the game against Germany in Norrköping. Hundreds of bodies were strewn in and around the station waiting for the early morning train. There were bodies on benches, half in bushes and lying in the middle of the road. A policeman woke one of the troops with his foot.

'You must get up. You cannot sleep here.'

'Why not?' the guy protested, 'there's people sleeping everywhere. Why are you bothering me?'

'Because the tram cars start in 5 minutes,' the helpful policeman explained. 'Your legs are on the tram lines.'

But it was the train journey which sticks in my mind. This was when Crazy Jimmy stopped the train. The train had just set off for Gothenburg, a journey of between three and four hours and the catering staff had obviously not anticipated a party in full swing. All the drink on board was soon purchased and consumed. 'I'm sorry sir, but you have drunk all the beer. We have nothing left,' the waiter explained to Jimmy. 'Well, you'll just need to stop and pick up more,' was Jimmy's reply. The problem was that this was an express train with no scheduled stops. There then began a prolonged period of negotiation with the head guard. Jimmy's perseverance won the day and the train made an unscheduled stop to replenish the exhausted bar.

Back in Gothenburg that afternoon in '92 in the company of Crazy Jimmy and Paddy McLaughlin the mood was reflective as we sat in the upper bar of the floating boat. Not much was being said. Scotland were out after an heroic performance against West Germany, then the reigning World Champions. We'd had a hard few days and were building up for one last pull against the CIS. Paddy broke the silence. 'Did anyone see that?' he asked casually. 'See what?'. 'Just keep your eye on that window there.' Nothing happened. 'Give it time,' says Paddy. A few minutes later: 'What the fuck was that?' as a guy in a kilt flew down past the window then a second or two later flew back up again, his kilt around his head.

I had noticed the big crane next to the boat during the past week, but I hadn't realised it was for bungee jumping.

This was some of the guys taking a well earned rest from the big beer tent positioned just a short stroll from the Avenue. One person who was certainly not bungee jumping was Mad Dog. Mad Dog only ventured out the beer tent to attend the matches. The organisers initially tried to shut the tent for a few hours early in the morning, but found on their return that Mad Dog had stormed the tent and showed no sign of leaving. The organisers then made the wise decision not to bother attempting to shut at all and opened round the clock.

More recently big Davie Lewis had a strange experience in a beer tent. This was in Vienna at the start of Scotland's qualifying campaign for France '98. Fans were pleasantly surprised to find a large beer tent right in the city centre square. There was a great atmosphere, bands and plenty of lederhosen clad locals mixing with the Tartan Army. We thought it was great that the Austrians had been so thoughtful and had taken the time to welcome us to their city like this. It wasn't until a couple of days later that we discovered that the celebrations had nothing to do with Scotland's visit. It was a centenary anniversary of the Vienna Fire Service.

In the tent big Davie fell asleep on one of the long beer tables as the festivities carried on around him. He woke up the following morning, a dog licking his hand, to find the tent gone. He was still on the table which by this time was the only thing left from the night before. Everything else had been lifted and the tent had been dismantled. There was big Davie in the middle of Vienna's main square with people going about their daily business wondering why a Scotsman in great highland plaid was lying stretched out sound asleep on a table.

Austria figured significantly in Scotland's qualification for the Finals in France. Many of us thought that the 2:1 defeat in Sweden in April 1997 might be the end of our bid as we were no longer in the driving seat. But Austria's later defeat of Sweden in Vienna put Scotland's destiny back into our own hands. There were three games to go: an away and a home match against Belarus and a final home game against the Latvians. Win all three and it looked likely that Scotland would qualify automatically as best second placed team or better.

So it was over to Belarus for the penultimate game in the qualifying campaign. A group of about twelve of us flew to Vilnius in Lithuania, arriving about 10pm with nowhere to stay and no idea about how we were going to get from Vilnius to Minsk.

We found a 'nice hotel', although Ian Mathieson chose to spend the night snuggled up in an downtown alleyway. You will not find this recommended, even in the *Rough Guides* to the Baltics. Ian received a few strange looks from his fellow travellers in the morning when he appeared looking more healthy that he probably should have.

We suspected Ian must have summoned dark forces for protection and since then he has been known as 'The Fiend.'

The transportation situation was soon sorted out. Once again, it was Tommy Madden to the rescue. A full size coach and a (normal sized) driver was hired and off we set. Chernobyl here we come. Tam Scones had taken the tasteless step of shaving his head in order to 'blend in' with the locals while most of the rest of us were content to fill our bags with medicines and cuddly toys to distribute in Minsk.

After making our way across the border, passing a line of stationary traffic that seemed to stretch for over

Belarus welcomes careful drivers.

2 miles, first stop was a duty fee shack. This was promptly bought. Totally cleared out. We left the deliriously happy owner locking up the premises, goodness knows for how long, and proceeded towards Minsk in the shadow of Chernobyl. But gas masks and blackened windows were not for this trusty band of Tartan Army. The weather was glorious and when the first lake was spotted this provided an occasion to stop, peel off and enjoy the warm, and possibly radiated, waters of Belarus. The driver obviously enjoyed

Bathing in the irradiated waters of Belarus. It's absolutely Baltic.

the spectacle of twelve Tartan Army, their kilts stretched end to end along the water's edge, splashing about with bottles of vodka and beer.

Gary McAllister scored the only goal of the match, which made up (a little bit) for his missed penalty against England the previous summer. The first set of three points were in the bag and Scotland were now just two steps away from France as the fans sang 'Here we glow, here we glow, here we glow...'

Big Davie Lewis and Dair MacGregor thought they had scored too on their way back from the match. Passing this big building, they looked up to see a group of women hanging out of a first floor window waving to them. So it was over a large fence, up a drainpipe and in through the window. There they found themselves surrounded by women wearing white smocks and closely cropped hair. They had gatecrashed the Minsk Mental Institute for Women.

Later that evening, I was in the company of The Fiend. We were searching for a quiet bar in the Hotel Belarus where we could just relax and reflect on the result and the last few days. A large group of wedding guests swept by on their way to the banquet dinner. We were spotted by the father of the bride who insisted that we join them, at least that is what we took him to mean. Sure enough, a couple of minutes later we found ourselves seated at the top table with the rest of the close family members, a wizened old lady in a headscarf who looked close to a hundred seated on my right. A fine and unexpected night was then had. It was good to observe the matrimonial customs of our Belarussian hosts. It was also good to get some solid grub down. The last we had seen that resembled (but only just) proper food had been the meal on the Lithuanian Airways flight.

The game in Minsk had been tight and the tension mounted as Scotland prepared to meet Belarus for the second time at Pittodrie. But there was drama ahead that nobody could have foreseen. Amidst the widespread hysteria that followed the death of Diana, the Government and large sections of the press turned on the SFA for planning to go ahead with the game on the same day as the funeral. Although the shops would be open in London at 2pm after the morning funeral, the SFA, and in particular Chief Executive Jim Farry, were vilified for planning to kick off the Belarus match at Aberdeen one hour later.

Relief and hope restored in Minsk.

The press turned savagely on Mr Jim Farry after he was asked to comment on the fact that Donald Dewar, Secretary of State for Scotland, had been trying to reach him concerning the game.

Mr Farry made some comment along the lines that as Colin Hendry was injured, Donald Dewar might be looking for a game in defence. In the face of mounting public pressure to cancel the game, the SFA eventually managed to reschedule the match for the following day, Sunday 7th September, 1997. It was disclosed on Friday 5th September that the SFA had come close to withdrawing from the World Cup altogether because of a range of behind the scenes difficulties in rearranging the match.

I know that many of the Tartan Army were outraged at the way the SFA was treated. Jim Briggs wrote to Mr Farry expressing the Edinburgh Tartan Army's support for the SFA's actions over the whole affair. Jim wanted Mr Farry to know that the vast majority of true fans were behind him and asked him to 'pass on our best wishes to the team and make sure that they know that, despite press reports that the Tartan Army will be subdued, we will be there at Pittodrie in full voice supporting Scotland.' Jim received a reply from Mr Farry telling him that his support was greatly appreciated.

Scotland's 4:1 home victory over the Belarussians was resounding and the fans were in fine voice. A few days later, the country as a whole was in fine voice when Scots expressed 'the settled will of the Scottish people' and voted overwhelmingly for the return of a Scottish Parliament after nearly 300 years of rule from London. The date, 11 September, was hugely significant. It was 700 years to the day that Sir William Wallace had defeated the invading English army at the Battle of Stirling Bridge and, along with Andrew Murray, was proclaimed Guardian of Scotland.

The final game against Latvia took place at a packed Parkhead. Scotland went one up towards the end of the first half, but it was not until late in the game that the result was put beyond doubt with Scotland's second goal. At that point you could feel the tension dissipate as it was blown away with resounding choruses of 'Que sera sera, whatever will be will be, we're going to gay

Paris, que sera sera.' The uninhibited singing became prophetic on the 4th of December when the World Cup draw was made. FIFA Vice President, Sepp Blatter, picked Scotland to face Brazil in the new St. Denis Stadium in Paris on the 10th of June, 1998.

Therefore, for only the second time in history, the first being back in 1974 in West Germany, Scotland would play Brazil as World Champions. And this time there would be one small

We're gonna celebrate, we're gonna celebrate…

difference. Bonnie Scotland versus Brazil would open the World Cup in France and over a quarter of the population of the globe would be watching. I watched the draw in the Vale Bar with Auld Davie as it took place live from Marseille. As it all began to sink in, he looked up with a twinkle in his eye: 'What was it you said you wanted for your birthday son?'

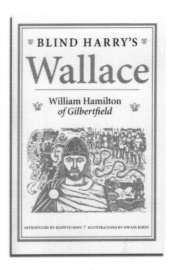

Blind Harry's Wallace

William Hamilton of Gilbertfield
Introduced by Elspeth King
ISBN 0 946487 33 2
PBK £7.50
ISBN 0 946487 43 X
HBK £15.00

The original story of the real braveheart, Sir William Wallace.

Racy, blood on every page, violently anglophobic, grossly embellished, vulgar and disgusting, clumsy and stilted, a literary failure, a great epic. Whatever the verdict on BLIND HARRY, this is the book which has done more than any other to frame the notion of Scotland's national identity. Despite its numerous 'historical inaccuracies', it remains the principal source for what we now know about the life of Wallace.

The novel and film Braveheart were based on the 1722 Hamilton edition of this epic poem. Burns, Wordsworth, Byron and others were greatly influenced by this version 'wherein the old obsolete words are rendered more intelligible', which is said to be the book, next to the Bible, most commonly found in Scottish households in the eighteenth century. Burns even admits to having 'borrowed... a couplet worthy of Homer' directly from Hamilton's version of BLIND HARRY to include in 'Scots wha hae'.

Elspeth King, in her introduction to this, the first accessible edition of BLIND HARRY in verse form since 1859, draws parallels between the situation in Scotland at the time of Wallace and that in Bosnia and Chechnya in the 1990s. Seven hundred years to the day after the Battle of Stirling Bridge, the 'Settled Will of the Scottish People' was expressed in the devolution referendum of 11 September 1997. She describes this as a landmark opportunity for mature reflection on how the nation has been shaped, and sees BLIND HARRY'S WALLACE as an essential and compelling text for this purpose.

The Bannockburn Years

William Scott
ISBN 0 946487 34 0
PBK £7.95

This is a love story, at the time of Scotland's greatest success.

How did the Scots win the War of Independence, against a neighbour ten times as powerful?

Did the Scots have a secret weapon at their disposal?

Was the involvement of women a deciding factor?

Should Scotland now become independent?

These questions lie at the heart of the medieval manuscript by John Bannatyne of Bute, genius, commander of the Scottish archers at Bannockburn, and eye-witness of Robert Bruce's heroic leadership.

A present day solicitor is asked to stand for the independence party in an election. In a client's will, he stumbles across reference to a manuscript of value to the Nation State of Scotland which he tracks down to the Island of Bute.

Is the document authentic? In the course of his investigation, involving a WWII fighter-pilot, the solicitor also discovers his answer to the question: should Scotland be independent now? Written with pace and passion, William Scott has devised an original vehicle for looking at the future of Scotland. He presents, for the first time, a convincing explanation of how the victory at Banockburn was achieved, with a rigorous examination of the history as part of the story.

Winner of the 1997 Constable Trophy, the premier award in Scotland for an unpublished novel, this book offers new insights to both the general and academic reader, sure to provoke further discussion and debate.

LUATH GUIDES TO SCOTLAND

South West Scotland
Tom Atkinson
ISBN 0 946487 04 9 PBK £4.95

The Lonely Lands
Tom Athinson
ISBN 0 946487 10 3 PBK £4.95

The Empty Lands
Tom Atkinson
ISBN 0 946487 13 8 PBK £4.95

Roads to the Isles
Tom Atkinson
ISBN 0 946487 01 4 PBK £4.95

Highways and Byways in Mull and Iona
Peter Macnab
ISBN 0 946487 16 2 PBK £4.25

NATURAL SCOTLAND

Wild Scotland
James McCarthy
ISBN 0 946487 37 5 PBK £7.50

An Inhabited Solitude: Scotland – Land and People
James McCarthy
ISBN 0 946487 30 8 PBK £6.99

Rum: Nature's Island
Magnus Magnusson
ISBN 0 946487 32 4 PBK £7.95

WALK WITH LUATH

Mountain Days & Bothy Nights
Dave Brown and Ian Mitchell
ISBN 0 946487 15 4 PBK £7.50

The Joy of Hillwalking
Ralph Storer
ISBN 0 946487 28 6 PBK £7.50

Walks in the Cairngorms
Ernest Cross
ISBN 0 946487 09 X P8K £3.95

Short Walks in the Cairngorms
Ernest Cross
ISBN 0 946487 23 5 PBK £3.95

BIOGRAPHY

On the Trail of Robert Service
Wallace Lockhart
ISBN 0 946487 24 3 PBK £7.95

Come Dungeons Dark
John Taylor Caldwell
ISBN 0 946487 19 7 PBK £6.95

Bare Feet and Tackety Boots
Archie Cameron
ISBN 0 946487 17 0 PBK £7.95

HUMOUR/HISTORY

Old Scotland New Scotland
Jeff Fallow
ISBN 0 946487 40 5 PBK £6.99

SOCIAL HISTORY

The Crofting Years
Francis Thompson
ISBN 0 946487 06 5 PBK £5.95

MUSIC AND DANCE

Highland Balls and Village Halls
Wallace Lockhart
ISBN 0 946487 12 X PBK £6.95

Fiddles and Folk
Wallace Lockhart
ISBN 0 946487 38 3 PBK £7.95

FOLKLORE

The Supernatural Highlands
Francis Thompson
ISBN 0 946487 31 6 PBK £8.99

POETRY

The Jolly Beggars or 'Love and Liberty'
Robert Burns
ISBN 0 946487 02 2 HB £8.00

Poems to be Read Aloud
selected and introduced by
Tom Atkinson
ISBN 0 946487 00 6 PBK £5.00

Luath Press Limited
committed to publishing well written books worth reading

LUATH PRESS takes its name from Robert Burns, whose little collie Luath (*Gael.*, swift or nimble) tripped up Jean Armour at a wedding and gave him the chance to speak to the woman who was to be his wife and the abiding love of his life. Burns called one of *The Twa Dogs* Luath after Cuchullin's hunting dog in Ossian's *Fingal*.
Luath Press grew up in the heart of Burns country, and now resides a few steps up the road from Burns' first lodgings in Edinburgh's Royal Mile.

Luath offers you distinctive writing with a hint of unexpected pleasures.

Most UK bookshops either carry our books in stock or can order them for you. To order direct from us, please send a £sterling cheque, postal order, international money order or your credit card details (number, address of cardholder and expiry date) to us at the address below. Please add post and packing as follows: UK – £1.00 per delivery address; overseas surface mail – £2.50 per delivery address; overseas air-mail – £3.50 for the first book to each delivery address, plus £1.00 for each additional book by airmail to the same address. If your order is a gift, we will happily enclose your card or message at no extra charge.

Luath Press Limited
543/2 Castlehill
The Royal Mile
Edinburgh EH1 2ND

Telephone: 0131 225 4326
Fax: 0131 225 4324
email: gavin.macdougall@luath.co.uk
Website: www.luath.co.uk